A MESSAGE FROM THE KEEPING KIDS SAFE FOUNDATION

We have reviewed hundreds of articles and books on the subject of preventing crimes against children. Our desire was to find a resource book for parents that could be read with their children emphasizing the importance of crime prevention, self esteem and honoring other peoples' rights as individuals.

In *Keeping Kids Safe*, we have found a guide that is full of simple, easy-to-follow steps that parents can take to help ensure their children's safety while highlighting the significance of developing a child's character.

The feedback we have received from parents has been very positive. Not only does this book give parents pointers on how to teach their children to protect themselves, it also encourages family discussions on other difficult topics such as drugs and dealing with the opposite sex.

Whether you are involved with the book as a corporate sponsor, a school district, an organization or as a concerned parent, we think you'll agree that *Keeping Kids Safe* is an excellent guide for parents raising children in today's world.

We wish to acknowledge and thank Guardian Press for allowing us the opportunity to offer this outstanding book at cost.

To learn more about the Keeping Kids Safe Foundation and its efforts on behalf of children, please visit our Web site at **www.kksf.org**.

WHAT EDUCATORS ARE SAYING ABOUT *KEEPING KIDS SAFE*

"The book is a helpful tool in the ongoing struggle to ensure the safety of our nation's children."

--Michael Casserly, Executive Director,
Council of Great City Schools
Washington, D.C.

"This book could be fundamental to the safety of children. It has my wholehearted support and endorsement."

--Joseph A. Fernandez
Former Chancellor New York City Schools and
Superintendent of Dade County, Florida,
Public Schools

"This easy-to-read book offers numerous 'what you can do' suggestions for teachers and parents."

--Bailey T. Stewart
Senior Executive Director
Dade County, Florida, Public Schools

"The book is a timely, needed informational guide which will help our schools in dealing with issues of crime, school safety, and secure school facilities."

--Lynn St. James
Chief Education Officer
Chicago Public Schools

"Your book has my strongest support and endorsement."

--Rod Paige
Superintendent of Schools
Houston Independent School District

KEEPING KIDS SAFE
Effective and Easy Steps to Protect Your Kids Against Crime

Published by Guardian Press, PMB #225, 10924 Grant Road, Houston, TX 77070, phone (281) 955-9855.

Email: rwble@ev1.net
Web: www.guardianpress.com

First Edition September, 1995
Second Printing June, 1996
Third Printing March, 1997
Fourth Printing November, 1997
Fifth Printing July, 1999
Sixth Printing September, 1999

ISBN 0-9632355-8-3
Printed in the United States of America

Library of Congress Catalog Card Number: 94-96799

Important Notice:

Crime prevention techniques cited in this book were obtained from various outside sources, including, but not limited to, federal, state and local law enforcement officials and crime prevention experts. We believe the information to be accurate and reliable. However, we do not warrant the accuracy or reliability of the information contained herein. Furthermore, the publisher makes no guarantees of results from the use of information contained herein. We assume no liability in connection with either the information contained in this book or the crime prevention suggestions made. Moreover, we would caution that it cannot be assumed that every acceptable crime prevention procedure is contained in this book. Obviously, abnormal or unusual situations or your individual circumstances may require further or additional procedures.

KEEPING KIDS SAFE

EFFECTIVE AND EASY STEPS TO PROTECT YOUR KIDS AGAINST CRIME

Richard W. Eaves
and
Richard L. Bloom

GUARDIAN PRESS

CONTENTS

ACKNOWLEDGMENTS

Guardian Press would like to thank the following organizations whose cooperation, information and suggestions helped make this book possible.

- Federal Bureau of Investigation,
  U.S. Department of Justice

- Keeping Kids Safe Foundation,
  Carmel, California

- National Center for Missing and Exploited
  Children, Arlington, Virginia

- National Crime Prevention Council,
  Washington, D.C.

INTRODUCTION

Most parents who read this book can look back on their childhood and recall carefree days that seemed to last forever. We had the freedom to go out and play, often until dark, without the need for constant adult supervision. It was not uncommon for young children to be sent off to school with only the warning, "Look both ways before you cross the street." Yes, there was a time when kids actually walked to school by themselves. Those days now seem idyllic, very different from the lives our own children face.

Many parents wouldn't dare send their kids off to school alone, or without a laundry list of precautions and warnings. We certainly can't let our kids go out to play without some form of adult supervision or control. We can barely leave older kids unsupervised in the supposed sanctity of our homes. Crime has robbed our kids of their childhood and its precious innocence.

The world must seem a bleak and forbidding place for kids today, and not just those living in the inner-city in constant fear of street gangs, drug dealers, drive-by shootings, burglars, muggers and rapists. Increased law enforcement in many large cities has driven criminals to suburban and rural areas, the very places middle-class Americans fled to escape the problems of crime. Now burglar bars and security warning signs are part of the suburban landscape. There simply is no such thing as a "totally safe neighborhood." As sad as it may sound, your children are at risk every day of their lives. While it's impossible to provide for their safety and well-being each minute of the day, you can do the next best thing: teach your children how to protect themselves.

Children must be trained from a very early age about the dangers they face. Sexual abuse, abduction, child prostitution, pornography, mugging, murder and more are all realities in our world. And there's always the possibility that your kids may have to face them one day. The proper training could be the key to their survival.

Crime is a very unpleasant topic for parents to discuss with their kids. Hopefully, this book will give you the kind of information that will make the task less imposing. Safety training doesn't have to be frightening. In fact, it can even be fun when various games, skits and activities are integral parts of the lessons. Just as you teach your kids about the perils of fire and traffic, you can also teach them about the dangers of crime.

The suggestions that follow will give you pointers on things you can do now. How you carry them out will be determined in large part by your skills as a parent and your philosophy on raising kids. Some experts believe that parents should rule the household as benevolent monarchies. The children do whatever the parents say. Others believe in taking a more democratic approach and letting the kids have a voice in matters that concern them.

Regardless of their philosophy, however, almost all experts agree that kids need rules and restrictions. And as parents know, all children will push any rule to the limit. Even the best of kids can have a rebellious streak as they begin to assert their independence. That's very normal. However, some of the things kids do in the process can put them in danger. You should never assume that your child is bright enough, mature enough or well-behaved enough to handle all situations. The fact is, many criminals are shrewd and devious enough to fool any child who hasn't had the proper training.

In this book, we have attempted to provide the vital information parents need to better educate themselves about the problems of crime so that they can effectively train their children. It's a responsibility that could be critical to the safety and well-being of their kids.

Contrary to some beliefs, talking about crime will not scare children to the point of paranoia. Fear in small degrees is not all bad. Being afraid to do certain things may keep a child from harm. On the other hand, a child who has a bad experience certainly isn't stronger for it. Teaching your kids self-protection skills (mental, not physical), can make them stronger and more self-confident.

THE FUNDAMENTALS

Can you be overly protective of your kids? Considering the thousands of children who turn up missing, exploited, mugged or murdered every day, it's doubtful. Parents are right to be fearful about the safety of their children.

As a parent, you have the ultimate responsibility for nurturing and caring for your kids. You and you alone can decide what is best for them. It cannot be left to the schools, the church or the government.

We believe the suggestions that follow are fundamental to the safety of your children. Various civil liberty experts and parenting professionals might disagree with some of the methods advocated here. Others will agree wholeheartedly, as will most crime prevention and law enforcement officials. They know full well the importance of parental involvement and the exercise of parental authority, from infancy to adulthood.

The objective of safety training is not to smother your children or shelter them from the harsh realities of our world. All kids must have a degree of freedom and independence, especially as they grow older. But what they need equally is the knowledge that there are bad people in this world who will do them harm, and that what you are doing is designed to protect them from those people. Bear in mind that few emotional scars from childhood are as deep or as difficult to heal as those that come from being a victim of crime.

1. Build Your Child's Self-Esteem.

Many kids who are exploited by criminals often are described as having strong needs for attention, affection and approval. They generally feel isolated and left out. This greatly increases their vulnerability. On the other hand, children who have a compelling sense of self-worth are much more difficult to exploit. So what can you do to help build self-esteem in your kids? Essentially, there are four things you can give your kids to build their sense of self-worth: love, time, discipline and acceptance.

Most of the time, it's very easy to love your kids. Other times, it's not so easy. It's hard to show your love for a child who is constantly rude, obnoxious and surly, like many are during adolescence. It's a paradox, but when kids are the most difficult to love is the very time they need your love the most. Parents who stick with their kids during the rebellious and antagonistic phases as well as the sweet and innocent ages are building a strong base of self-esteem for their kids.

One reflection of your love is the time you spend with your kids. Simply put, your children need an awful lot of your time, and that's not always easy to provide. Of course, they need some "quality time" when your kids are the center of attention. They need you to be there at the school play, the ball game and so forth. But they also need some "mundane time" when you simply are there, available if they happen to need you. This doesn't mean you have to give them your undivided attention. Just a parent's presence in the household often is enough for most kids. Sometimes, we get so caught up in our careers and outside interests that we lose sight of how little time we actually spend with our kids. Nothing is more difficult than finding adequate time for our kids, but few things in life are more important.

Disciplining your kids also is a daunting task. Setting rules fairly and sticking to them consistently can test the skills of any parent. No matter what boundaries and restrictions you place on your kids, they will constantly be probing and pushing to go beyond them. That's normal. But kids who are required to follow the rules and stay within the boundaries set by their parents, no matter how much children may seem to resist, feel loved and important.

The issue of acceptance, or approval, is possibly one of the toughest of all. It's natural for parents to have high hopes for their kids. We'd all like to have our kids excel academically, be the star player or the class president. We have great expectations for our kids, but more often than not, they don't measure up to the standards we set. One of the keys to building self-esteem is accepting your child for what he or she is. Every child is an individual with unique personality traits. Each has weaknesses as well as strengths and learns at different speeds and in different ways. We certainly should expect our kids to try as hard as they possibly can and give it their very best. But whether they make straight A's in the process or barely pass, our approval of their efforts and our validation of their self-worth is essential to their well-being.

WHAT YOU CAN DO

❑ Spend as much time with your kids as you possibly can. If you have more than one child, try to budget your time so that you can spend a certain amount of time alone with each child. Although this may prove difficult given the busy schedule of most people, it is important enough in the development of your children to forego other activities in your life if necessary.

❑ Always try to be there for the significant things in your children's lives. The school play, the spelling bee, the awards ceremony, etc., are important milestones that children naturally want to share with their parents.

❑ Set clear rules and stick to them. But try not to be overly harsh with punishment. All kids are going to make mistakes, and none will follow all the rules all the time. Set limits in a firm but loving way.

❑ Take the positive approach. Praise your kids for their good choices instead of admonishing them for bad choices. All kids are going to make mistakes. Help them learn from their missteps by pointing them in the right direction.

❑ Respect your children's feelings. Never make light of their doubts, fears, ideas or notions.

❑ Encourage achievement without being pushy. Your kids should know that you expect their very best effort, but that you understand their limits. Praise their accomplishments. Never shame them for their failures.

❑ Share your own beliefs and values with your kids. Talk and listen to your kids to help give them a greater sense of self-importance.

SUPPLEMENTAL READING

Six Vital Ingredients of Self-Esteem, by Betty B. Youngs.

Self-Esteem: The Key to Your Child's Well-Being, by Harris Clemes and Reynold Bean

Your Child's Self-Esteem, by Dorothy Corhille Briggs

Freedom to Fly: Activities for Building Self-Worth, by Chris Brewer

The Power of Encouragement, by Stephanie Marston

2. *Know What's Going on in Your Kids' Lives.*

Stay abreast of the things that are important to your kids: who their friends are, what kinds of clothes they think are "in," where they like to go for entertainment, the music they enjoy, the games they play, what they are doing at school and so forth. Of course, this will be easier with young children since they love to share their thoughts and experiences with other family members. But as kids get older, especially as they enter adolescence, they are less willing to open up to their parents. With some tactful and delicate probing, however, it is possible to communicate with your kids without seeming to snoop or pry. The more you know about what's happening with your kids, the better you will be able to help steer them clear of potentially dangerous situations.

WHAT YOU CAN DO

❑ Get to know your children's teachers, coaches, and counselors. Visit your child's school routinely, not just during open houses, school plays, etc.

❑ Try to attend your child's after-school activities or classes. If you can't be there, try to get a family member, relative or trusted friend to attend in your place.

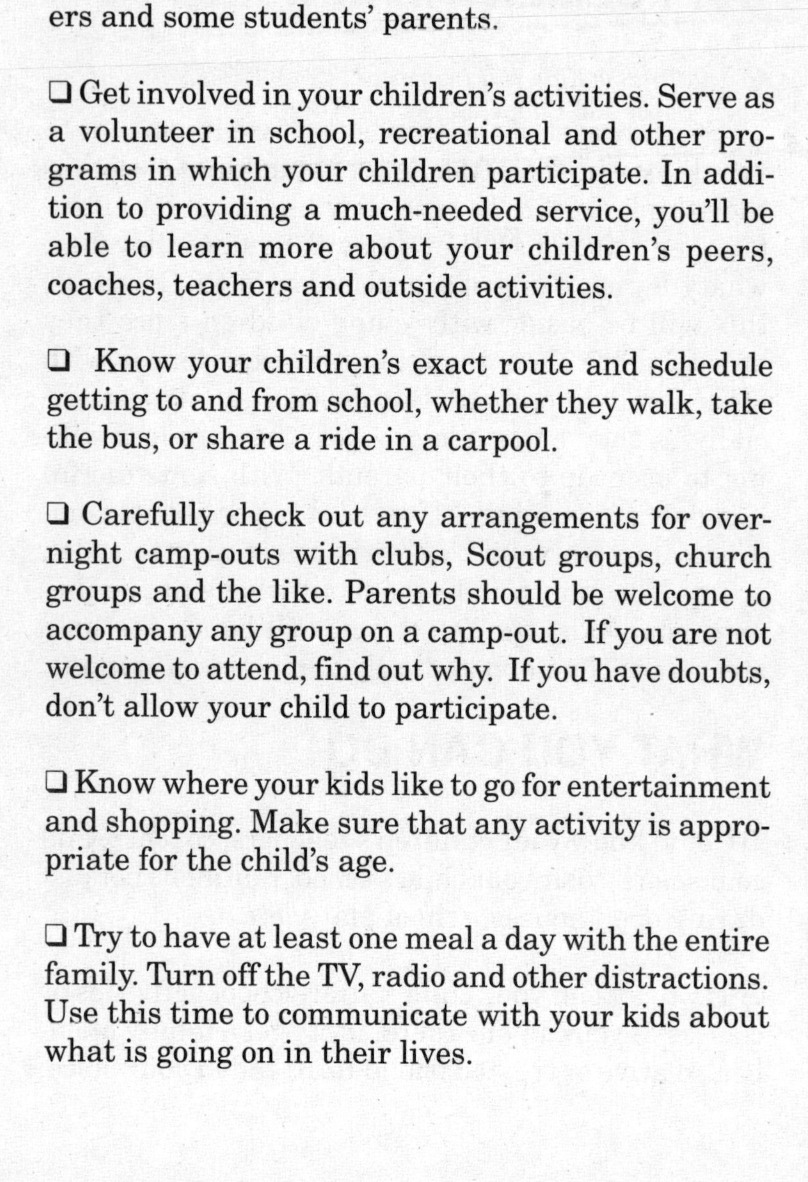

❑ Avoid giving blanket permission for a school to take your children off the school grounds. You should know exactly where your child is going and why before you give permission. Chaperones should include teachers and some students' parents.

❑ Get involved in your children's activities. Serve as a volunteer in school, recreational and other programs in which your children participate. In addition to providing a much-needed service, you'll be able to learn more about your children's peers, coaches, teachers and outside activities.

❑ Know your children's exact route and schedule getting to and from school, whether they walk, take the bus, or share a ride in a carpool.

❑ Carefully check out any arrangements for overnight camp-outs with clubs, Scout groups, church groups and the like. Parents should be welcome to accompany any group on a camp-out. If you are not welcome to attend, find out why. If you have doubts, don't allow your child to participate.

❑ Know where your kids like to go for entertainment and shopping. Make sure that any activity is appropriate for the child's age.

❑ Try to have at least one meal a day with the entire family. Turn off the TV, radio and other distractions. Use this time to communicate with your kids about what is going on in their lives.

❑ Remember that communication involves talking *and* listening.

SUPPLEMENTAL READING

How to Talk So Kids Will Listen & Listen So Kids Will Talk, by Adele Faber and Elaine Mazlish

Teaching Your Children Values, by Linda and Richard Eyre

Raising Responsible Kids, by Karen Feiden

Making Children Mind Without Losing Yours,by Dr. Kevin Leman

3. *Listen to What Your Kids Are Saying in Their Words and Actions.*

Children who aren't listened to or do not have their needs met in the home are sometimes more vulnerable to exploitation. Therefore, it is vitally important for parents to learn to communicate with their children in a positive manner.

Younger children are more likely than teens to openly express their fears and problems, but not always. Sometimes kids will try to tell you something by the questions they ask. Other times, changes in their behavior can be signals that something isn't quite right. Sudden swings in eating or sleeping habits, frequent nightmares, a reluctance to go to school, becoming quiet and withdrawn—these are just a few possible problem signs that deserve your immediate attention.

Also, if you have a child in day-care who becomes overly concerned about his or her genitalia or has recurring dreams or nightmares about them, you should immediately remove the child from the day-care center while you investigate the situation. These might be signals that your child is being physically or sexually abused. If you aren't paying close attention to what your kids are trying to say, you might not realize that they are crying out for help.

WHAT YOU CAN DO

❑ Watch for physical signs that something may be wrong in your kids' lives. Genital or urinary problems, recurrent headaches and/or upset stomach, stomach cramps, bruises and cuts are a few of the possible symptoms. These conditions should be checked by a doctor at once. If you believe there is physical or sexual abuse involved, you should notify the police or school officials so they can investigate further.

❑ Watch for sudden changes in eating or sleeping habits. If kids begin to refuse their favorite foods or lose their appetites altogether, have trouble sleeping or wake up in the middle of the night, have recurring bad dreams or nightmares, or begin to exhibit a fear of the dark, you should try to determine the causes. If you're unsuccessful, you should seek professional child counseling.

❑ Watch for sudden changes in your child's behavior. Some possible warning signs: your child becomes shy or withdrawn; regresses to earlier patterns of behavior; seems depressed; appears preoccupied about something; exhibits a reluctance to go to school; starts having problems at school; attempts to run away from home; becomes passive and uncaring. If your child exhibits any of these conditions, you should immediately try to get to the bottom of the situation. If you're unsuccessful, you should seek professional child counseling.

❑ Try to set aside some time each day to talk and listen to your kids. This can be done at dinner, while doing the dishes, helping with homework, even while watching certain television shows.

❑ Take an interest in what your kids tell you. Never make light of any fear or concern your child expresses. Do not accuse your child of making up a situation. Take it seriously, and get to the bottom of it at once.

❑ Try to avoid lecturing, preaching and nagging. Keep the lines of communication open. Let your kids do as much of the talking as possible. Offer your opinions and suggestions whenever they seem appropriate.

❑ Talk *with* your kids, not down to them. Be receptive and open so that your kids will feel comfortable enough to talk to you about any topic.

❑ Don't treat sex as a taboo subject. If your child is ever molested, he or she may be reluctant to tell you about it if sex is a forbidden topic of discussion in the family.

SUPPLEMENTAL READING

Sex is Not a Four-Letter Word! Talking Sex with Your Children Made Easier, by Patricia Martens Miller.

4. *Fingerprint Your Kids.*

Although fingerprinting in itself doesn't protect your kids against abductors, molesters or other criminals, it definitely makes it easier for the police to trace and identify missing children. Most law enforcement agencies throughout the nation strongly encourage the practice. However, some civil liberty groups see fingerprinting as an invasion of a child's privacy. As the parent, you must decide whether your children's safety is more important than their right to privacy. We strongly favor fingerprinting, although we do recommend that you, not the police, retain the records.

The simplest procedure is to have the police department or community service group fingerprint your kids. You can call the Crime Prevention Division of your local police or sheriff's department to get more information. Ideally, there should be only one set of fingerprints taken and retained by you, the parent or guardian.

If you feel uncomfortable involving the police, you can purchase a kit that allows you to fingerprint your kids at home. Several reputable organizations sell these kits at a nominal price. If you do it yourself, make sure you get a set of good-quality prints. This may entail repeating the procedure several times.

But keep trying until you get it right. A set of prints that can't be read won't do the police much good.

WHAT YOU CAN DO

❑ Contact your local police department or sheriff's department to find out the procedure for having your children fingerprinted.

❑ Keep the fingerprints in your possession, ideally in a personal file you keep for each of your children.

5. *Always Have a Recent Photo, Video and Current Information on Your Kids.*

When a child is missing, what the police need most is an accurate description, and nothing fits the bill better than a recent photo or video. Ideally, you should take a full-face photograph of your child every three months. This is particularly true of younger kids whose physical appearance can change rapidly. It's very difficult for police to look for a five-year-old when all they have is a photo of the child at age two.

Who knows? You may need the photograph to conduct your own search. In the case of teenagers, some police departments will not even begin to search until the teen has been missing at least three days. You don't want to wait that long. If you have a recent photograph, you will be able to quickly produce and distribute flyers to help begin the search.

Along with a current photograph, keep a list of your child's physical characteristics, personality traits, even a lock of hair. It's also a good idea to have dental and medical records in your possession. It stands to reason that the faster you can provide accurate information to the police, the better chance they will have of finding or identifying your child.

WHAT YOU CAN DO

❑ Take a good quality full-face photo from the front and side every three months. It's also a good idea to take a full body photograph once a year. If you can do so, transfer photos to digital files that can be stored on a compuer floppy disc.

❑ Keep photos, dental and medical records, and a lock of you child's hair in a file along with the child's fingerprints. Make sure you keep the file in a secure place.

❑ You should try to weigh and measure your kids every three months during their "growth" years to keep information as up-to-date as possible.

❑ Make a list of any physical marks or personality traits that you feel would aid the police in locating your child if he or she were missing.

❑ If possible, put a copy of all information, including photographs and fingerprints, on a computer disc. This will make it more convenient to update periodically. More importantly, it will also make it easier to upload to the Internet in the event you need to use the Web to post information about a missing child. You can also E-mail such files directly to police departments. However, do not store these files on your Web site, since it's too easy for hackers to break in and steal information about your child. Store your information on a floppy disc instead.

❑ Keep all information related to each of your children in a separate file. Other information the file should contain includes:

- A copy of your child's birth certificate
- Your child's blood type
- A list of medical problems that might require medication
- A list of existing allergies
- Eye glass prescription and frame type
- A current directory of school and neighbohood friends
- A current directory of teachers, coaches, doctors, counselors, etc.
- A description of the child's interests and recreational activities
- A list of places and phone numbers where the child frequently goes
- The child's current distress word (see page 120)

SUPPLEMENTAL READING

My Child is Missing. How to Protect Your Child from Abduction and What to Do If It Happens, by Robert Poe

6. Get to Know Your Kids' Friends and Their Parents.

You would certainly want to know if your kids were hanging out with friends who use drugs or alcohol. Or if their parents are abusive or use or sell drugs. Try to encourage your kids to resist befriending other kids in such situations. Of course, you can't pick and choose friends for your kids, especially teenagers, but you can possibly influence their choices. By instilling the right values in their younger years, you are laying a solid foundation for their choices in later years.

At the very least, try to know the names, addresses and phone numbers of your children's friends. If possible, get a photo from the friend's parents. Try to network with other parents to keep a better handle on what is going on with your own kids. Know their haunts and hang-outs. All this information can be vital if you have to locate a missing child.

WHAT YOU CAN DO

❑ Try to get to know the parents of your children's friends. Invite them over for coffee or another casual meeting. You don't have to be friends with the parents, but you definitely should know something about them. If you feel any reservations about the parents, ask some of your friends or acquaintances what they know of them. You are not trying to be a snoop or a gossip; rather, you are trying to get information that may affect the safety of your child. This is your right and responsibility. Discourage the friendship if you feel uncomfortable with the parents.

❑ Do not let your children visit the home of a friend until you have met the friend and feel comfortable with the association.

❑ When your child visits a friend's home for the first time, insist that you take your child. You should expect the parent to invite you inside. If you feel uncomfortable with the situation, politely indicate that you have a change of plans and that your child will not be able to stay. Do not leave your child if you have the slightest reservation.

❑ Do not let your children sleep over with a friend until you have met the friend's parents and feel comfortable with your child spending time in their household.

❑ Make sure you have an understanding with the friend's parents about what activities are acceptable or unacceptable, where your child is allowed to go if an outing is involved, and where the parents can notify you in case of an emergency. If they are responsible parents, they will certainly understand your caution.

❑ Network with the parents of your children's friends. Encourage other parents to inform you of any problem they might have with their children, your children or any friends they might have in common. Here again, the intent is not to snoop, but to stay informed and head off serious problems.

❑ Set guidelines for the "friends" your kids are allowed to bring home. Some teens have been known to pose as friends only to gain access to your house to case it for a burglary.

❑ Discourage your kids from socializing with any kids you suspect of being gang members. There have been cases where innocent youngsters were killed or injured in gang warfare simply because they were at a party or other gathering attended by a gang member. A few telltale signs that a kid *might* be involved with gangs could include the following:

• Has little or no parental supervision

• Makes poor grades and/or has frequent discipline problems at school

• Wears gang clothing (colors, hats, sweat suits, ball caps, flags, insignias, bandanas, etc.) or has drawings of gang insignia on clothing

• Has tatoos, either hand-drawn or professionally done, on the body

• Speaks in gang vernacular

7. Monitor Your Kids' Music, TV Viewing and Video Games.

If you disapprove of certain music or lyrics, the content of a television show or the violence of a particular video game, take action. This, too, is one of your rights and responsibilities as a parent. Study after study has shown that children are indeed influenced by what they see and hear in the media. Television cartoons that are linked to toys are particularly influential. Psychological studies indicate that when kids play with such toys, they are inclined to reenact the violent scenarios they have seen on television.

Some video games also lead to violent behavior. Many are gory and sexist and often require the player to kill an opponent. Furthermore, these games are so technologically advanced that they approach "virtual reality," making it more difficult for kids to separate the violence in the game from real life.

Although some experts disagree on the amount of control you should exert over your kids' music and video choices, most experts agree on the fact that kids need limitations and boundaries. Set them fairly, then stick to them. Your own instincts as a parent are usually the best guidelines.

WHAT YOU CAN DO

❑ Set limits on the amount of television your kids can watch without your supervision.

❑ Schedule some regular viewing times to watch television with your kids so you can discuss anything that seems frightening or inappropriate.

❑ Let your children know which programs you like and dislike and the reasons why. Be prepared to expect a peaked interest on their part regarding your dislikes.

❑ Be aware that the content of certain news programs contain as much gore and violence as many entertainment shows.

❑ If you feel that television and radio stations are broadcasting material that is inappropriate for your children, call or write the station with your protest. This is your right as a parent and citizen. Also, let the sponsor know.

❑ Read all warnings on video games. If at all possible, try to preview the game before you let your child buy it. Many stores now have preview copies that can be viewed before the game is purchased.

❑ Pay attention to all warnings about nudity, violence and inappropriate language provided by the broadcaster or included on video and music cassette packaging.

❑ Take the time to listen to records, cassettes and compact discs your kids purchase or borrow from friends. Some music lyrics can contain dangerous messages for your kids.

❑ Remember, as a parent, you have the right to censor what your children listen to, read and watch. However, the right of censorship does not extend to what others choose to see or hear. If you don't want your children exposed to certain programs or music, exercise your parental rights and responsibility to prohibit such material.

8. Monitor Your Kids' Possessions

Here again, some experts might argue that it's an invasion of privacy to go through your kids' personal property. Maybe they're right. But when you consider the proliferation of guns, drugs and other dangerous material to which your kids can be exposed (even at a very early age), a little detective work on your part may help keep your kids out of harm's way.

This is not to suggest that you become a snoop. Your kids definitely deserve some privacy, particularly in the confines of their own room. However, given the importance of your kids' safety, your need to know what is going on in their lives would seem to outweigh their right to complete privacy.

If you find items that you consider to be dangerous or harmful (guns, ammunition or other weapons; drugs or drug paraphernalia; alcohol or inhalants; pornography, especially that which depicts violence, children, bestiality or other behavior that seems aberrant to you), you should discuss the matter with your child to determine whether it is a deep-rooted problem or merely a curiosity. Of course, you should immediately confiscate any items that you feel are dangerous or inappropriate and explain why you are doing it.

Without question, this is a delicate issue, and you'll have to rely on your parental instincts as to the best way to handle it.

WHAT YOU CAN DO

❑ Explain to your kids that your actions are not a matter of your distrust, but rather your concern for their safety. Given the many potential dangers kids face in the world today, they are very likely to understand your actions so long as you are open and honest about them.

❑ Set rules and consistently stick to them about what is and is not appropriate for your kids to have in the house, including the confines of their rooms.

❑ Practice what you preach. Your kids might get the feeling that you have a double standard if you prohibit certain things in their lives in which you personally indulge. Remember, kids learn as much from our actions as from our words.

❑ Let your kids know that you do respect their privacy, but make them aware that your concern for their safety has to supersede all other rights.

❑ Encourage your kids to maintain a semblance of order and tidiness in their rooms. Make it known that you do inspect their room from time to time.

9. Be Aware of the Dangers on the Internet.

If you wanted to know how to make a pipe bomb using common household ingredients, how to make certain drug paraphernalia—even how to assassinate someone—you could find access to such information readily available on the Internet. So can your kids.

They can also find information from hate groups promoting violence, view sexually explicit materials, participate in chat room discussions that may include pedophiles and other sexual deviants, and play computer games that often depict extremely violent scenes. And, as the so-called "information highway" grows and expands, the spread of dangerous information is likely to increase.

Many parents, legislators and Internet Service Providers are concerned about the use of the Worldwide Web to sell and exchange pornography. Scenes depicting explicit sex acts are readily available to anyone with access to the Internet, including your kids. There also are a number of Web addresses that cater exclusively to buyers and sellers of child pornography.

While the dissemination of such material may be irresponsible, most of it is legal. Information on the Worldwide Web is protected by the free speech provisions of the Bill of Rights. The only way to prevent your kids from receiving such information is to monitor their computer activities as much as possible. In some cases, you can "block" Web sites and access them only with a key password. The same is true for bulletin boards or message services. It is advisable to carefully screen them and block those that you feel are inappropriate.

Also be aware that some computer "chat" lines have been used by molesters and abductors to lure youngsters into their clutches. Other criminal types have used bulletin boards to obtain information that has been used for everything from credit card fraud to burglaries.

Your best bet is to thoroughly check all computer information services and chat lines and cancel or block those that you feel are not suitable for your family.

WHAT YOU CAN DO

❑ Avoid letting kids use the computer in the privacy of their room. Try to keep your computer out in the open (in the living room, den or study) where you can better monitor what your kid is viewing.

❑ Check the menu of computer bulletin boards on your software program to try to identify any that are inappropriate for the age and interests of your kids.

❑ Periodically check the bookmarks on your Web

browser software to see which sites your kids have been visiting. If you know how to use the computer's "history" funtion, you can determine all the sites that have ever been visited from your computer.

❑ Check with your Internet Service Provider to determine if you can block bulletin boards and chat rooms that you think are unsuitable for your kids. This is often accomplished by assigning a password or other code that must be entered into the computer before certain Web sites can be accessed. These passwords probably are your first line of defense. However, if your child is proficient in computers, as many are, he or she may be able to circumvent or break the password code. If you're unable to block specific bulletin boards, your only choice may be to cancel the service altogether.

❑ Make inquiries among computer software retailers, computer enthusiasts, teachers and other parents about dangerous bulletin boards, chat lines, and Web sites to better identify the ones you feel are inappropriate.

❑ Consider installing "blocking software" on your computer. One such program, called NetNanny, has proved to be very effective in helping parents regulate what their kids see and do on the Internet. Using "key word" input from you, the parent, the software program will scan the Internet for web sites you deem inappropriate for your kids. The software will then block access to those sites on your computer.

10. Make Your Kids Aware of the Dangers of Sexual Abuse by Strangers.

Child molestation is one of the crimes that worries parents the most. And for good reason. It is one of the most hideous of all crimes. The best way to protect your kids against sexual abuse by strangers is to teach them to protect themselves. And in this matter, education is the best weapon. In educating your kids, however, you will have to walk a fine line between enlightening and frightening them. The fact that there are adults out there who will do them harm is hard for children to accept since they must rely on grown-ups for their safety and well-being.

WHO IS A STRANGER?

One of the most difficult challenges is helping children understand exactly who is a stranger and who is not. A stranger can be a man or a woman, even one as clean-cut and wholesome looking as the child's aunt or grandmother. Furthermore, a stranger isn't always someone unfamiliar to your child. A stranger might be someone your child sees every day, such as a school crossing guard, a custodian, store clerk, mail carrier or other adult your child recognizes on sight. Yet, in reality, they are all strangers.

You may be familiar with them, but you really don't know them. And neither do your kids.

You might explain to your child that, as a rule, a stranger is someone your family doesn't know well enough to invite into the home. You don't know where the stranger lives, his family, his children or any of his friends. While it is all right for the child to have polite exchanges with such a person, it is not appropriate to have lengthy conversations with him, and it is never acceptable to go off with such a person.

WHO IS A MOLESTER?

Another challenge to teaching your children the dangers of sexual abuse is overcoming our own stereotypical image of a child molester. We often picture such a person as a "dirty old man" in a raincoat lurking in the shadows. Such people probably do exist, but they hardly fit the typical profile of a sexual abuser.

The truth is, just about anyone can be a molester, and such a person cannot be readily identified on sight. However, there are several general guidelines that might, or might not, indicate that a person has the potential to be a molester. This person may have (1) been abused or molested as a child, (2) has few, if any friends in his own peer group, preferring instead the company of younger people, (3) is shy, passive or non-assertive, (4) is single and past the age of 30, (5) has a history of mental health problems, (6) may have a police record, and (7) performs adequately in a job requiring little initiative. Bear in mind that this is merely a profile. Just because a person exhibits any or all of these characteristics does not automatically make him a child molester. And some child molesters may not exhibit any of these characteristics.

Crime statistics indicate that nearly one-third of all convicted sex criminals were abused as children. The statistics also reveal that many sex offenders grew up in homes where sex was totally restricted, repressed and considered wrong and sinful. The majority of sexual abusers are relatively young, in their mid- to late-thirties. They generally are clean-cut, well-dressed and "normal" looking. There also is a significant number of adolescent abusers, plus a growing number of children who abuse younger children. Almost 90% of sexual abusers are males, but the number of reported female abusers has been on the increase over the last decade.

Psychologists define molesters as either fixated or regressive. The fixated molester's tendencies probably begin during adolescence, and his primary sexual orientation is toward children, usually boys. He very likely suffered some sort of sexual trauma in his childhood, such as being sexually abused himself. On the other hand, the regressive molester may have an otherwise normal sexual orientation toward women his own age. Some sort of stressful situation in his life leads him to molest children, usually young girls.

While the phrase "child snatcher" often is used in the same breath as "child molester," few children are actually snatched up and taken forcibly. Most kids are tricked or lured into the hands of molesters.

Such people usually are devious and cunning enough to talk a child into leaving willfully, sometimes using a trumped up story about a missing puppy or toy (see page 120). Unfortunately, it's difficult to identify such a person. He or she probably looks and seems to act like a perfectly normal person. The only defense a child has is to be very cautious around all strangers.

WHAT YOU CAN DO

❑ Make sure your kids fully comprehend exactly who a stranger is (even people we see every day can be strangers). Reinforce the idea that even strangers who look and act nice can sometimes be bad people.

❑ Explain that, while most adults are good people who wouldn't hurt kids, there are some grown-ups who would if they had the opportunity.

❑ Create a special "code word," known only to you and your children, to be used in emergency situations (see page 120).

❑ Teach young children that they are never to wander off alone (or even go off with a friend) without first getting your approval.

❑ Teach your children that under no circumstances are they to go off with a stranger, even if the stranger claims there is some sort of emergency involved. Your kids should know that is not appropriate for adults to ask children for help.

❑ To be on the safe side, make it a standing rule that your children must get your permission before they go off with anyone, period. Make sure they understand that they are not to leave the house, the school, the church, the store—not anywhere—without first getting your permission. Your child should know this rule applies to any stranger, whether it's a teacher, a preacher, the police, whomever. This rule should also apply to friends.

❑ Help your kids understand that they should always try to be polite, but at the same time, they should forcefully refuse to leave the premises with any stranger without first getting your approval.

❑ Make sure your kids understand the concept of "private parts" of the body (see page 51). They should understand that it is never okay for a person to touch them in these areas, even someone they know (unless it is a doctor or nurse administering health care with your consent).

❑ Make sure your kids know their home address and phone number, as well as your phone number at work and the number of a trusted friend or neighbor.

❑ Teach your kids how to use pay phones and other types of telephones. Make sure they know how to call for help. Teach them how to dial 911 or "0" in an emergency.

❑ Teach your kids exactly what to do if they get separated from you at the mall, an amusement park, parade, supermarket, etc. (see page 143).

❑ Keep all instructions as simple and concise as possible. Try to boil down instructions into key phrases and statements your child can understand. For example, when explaining what to do if confronted with a dangerous situation, you might rely on four key phrases:

"SAY NO!" if a stranger tries to touch you or get you to go away with him or her.

"RUN AWAY" as fast as you can. Go inside a store, a fire station, a restaurant, a gas station or some other place where there are people.

"YELL" things like,"This isn't my Mom/Dad! I'm being hurt!" as loudly you can to call attention to yourself and let other adults know you need help.

"TELL SOMEBODY" after you reach safety. That may help the police catch the stranger and prevent him or her from hurting other kids.

❑ As difficult as it might be, it's important to be able to discuss topics of a sexual nature with your kids and be open and honest about the subject. Kids are almost certain to be curious and raise questions about sex at some point in their development. It's vital to their mental and emotional health that they get the right answers from their parents.

SUPPLEMENTAL READING

For children ages 3 and up:

Strangers Don't Look Like the Big Bad Wolf, by Janis Buschman and Debbie Hunley

For school-age children:

Who Is a Stranger, And What Should I Do?, by Linda Walvoord Girard

Playing It Smart: What to Do When You're on Your Own, by Tova Navarra

For parents:

Victims. A Survival Guide for the Age of Crime, by Richard L. Bloom

Child Lures, by Kenneth Wooden

11. Make Your Kids Aware of the Dangers of Sexual Abuse by Acquaintances.

Between 60% and 75% of reported child sexual abuse cases are committed by an acquaintance: a family friend, a relative, a neighbor, a teacher, a live-in boyfriend—even a priest or minister. This makes it extremely difficult for children to recognize and avoid sexual abuse since these are usually the very people we teach our kids to respect. But kids must learn that it's all right to say "no" to sexual advances, even if it involves someone of authority.

Although the circumstances vary, when a child is sexually exploited by an acquaintance, the situation may develop gradually over a period of time and may involve subtle rather than physical force. Bribery, special secrets, threats and coercion are the most commonly used methods of drawing the child into the situation.

It's not unusual for such abuse to be recurring over a period of time. And it may take many different forms, from talking about things of a sexual nature, to exhibitionism, viewing pornography, fondling and/or oral/genital contact. All of these things constitute sexual abuse if the child involved is legally considered a minor (under the age of 16 in most states).

WHAT YOU CAN DO

❑ Discuss the "private parts" concept with your kids (see page 51). Your kids should know that no one has the right to touch them in these areas (the part of the body covered by a bathing suit for boys and girls). Teach your kids that this rule applies to anyone who tries to touch them.

❑ To make the training less stressful, use games, stories and role playing to help kids learn it's okay to say no to anyone who tries to touch them on private parts of the body (see page 53).

❑ Encourage your kids to follow their instincts. If any behavior by an adult acquaintance makes them feel weird or uncomfortable, it's probably inappropriate.

❑ Keep the lines of communication open with your kids so they feel comfortable talking to you about such matters.

❑ Never make light of any fears or concerns your child may express. Check them out at once!

❑ Be leery of any adult who likes to spend an inordinate amount of time with your child.

❑ Get involved in any sport or other activity in which your child participates. Be especially cautious with coaches and other leaders who do not have children of their own in the same group.

❑ Keep a close eye on any strong bond that develops between your child and an adult figure (an older cousin, uncle, teacher, coach, pastor, etc.). There have been numerous cases of children being sexually abused over long periods of time simply because the parents placed too much trust in an acquaintance.

❑ Avoid letting your child go on overnight trips alone with an adult acquaintance.

❑ Question your child about any money or gifts that are given by an adult. Unless you know for certain that the child has performed certain chores to earn the money, such gifts should be considered suspect.

❑ Never force your child to submit to unwanted hugs, kisses or other physical contact with acquaintances. Doing so could be sending conflicting messages to your child.

SUPPLEMENTAL READING

For school-age children:

It's Okay to Say Don't!, by Betty Boeghold (with illustrations by Carolyn Bracken)

No More Secrets for Me, by Oralee Wachter

12. Teach Your Kids the Meaning of "Private Parts" of the Body.

As a general rule, private parts of the body can be defined as those areas that normally are covered when a person wears a bathing suit. Children should know that these parts of the body are considered "private" because they are not to be touched or viewed by other people.

Teaching this concept to your child is a very delicate task. Many parents find it difficult to discuss sexually related subjects with their kids. However, if children are to learn about the dangers of sexual abuse and molestation, they must have an understanding of the parts of the body involved. But it must be done in a way that will not make the child fearful or overly concerned with his or her genitalia.

In offering such training to your kids, it's important to explain that there is nothing strange, unusual or "dirty" about these parts of the body. They are simply areas that we choose to keep private. Adults know that they are private, and only a bad person would try to touch a child on these parts of the body (the obvious exception is medical personnel who might have to touch these parts of the body during examinations or other medical procedures).

WHAT YOU CAN DO

❑ Try to keep all discussions as casual and natural as possible so as not to frighten or intimidate the child.

❑ Use "what if" games, make believe stories and role playing to discuss the issue.

❑ Use hand puppets or dolls to demonstrate the difference between good touching and bad touching. Lifelike dolls with removable clothing (Barbie, Ken, etc.) allow you to demonstrate the idea as part of your child's play.

❑ Children should understand that not only is it inappropriate for an adult to touch these parts of their body, but that it's also inappropriate for an adult to want a child to touch a grown-up's private parts.

SUPPLEMENTAL READING

For school-age kids:

Don't Touch Me There, by Oralee Wachter

13. Use Activities and Games to Teach Your Kids Safety Skills.

In the case of measles, mumps and other childhood diseases, most parents take the precaution of having their kids inoculated to prevent the disease. Teaching your kids the proper safety skills is not unlike vaccinating them against crime and violence. These "societal" diseases can be just as life threatening as medical diseases. In fact, in some segments of our society, homicide is the number one cause of death for teenagers.

Naturally, parents play a critical role in protecting their kids. Much of the crime and violence that occurs each day can be prevented when kids know (1) the proper safety skills and (2) how to satisfy their own needs without resorting to force. Many incidents which turn violent at school or in the streets probably could have been avoided if children had known how to back down from an argument and walk away from a confrontation or challenge.

When teaching your kids safety rules, it's very important to control your anxiety levels to minimize the fear you instill in your children. Giving your kids a descriptive account of what might happen if they don't follow their safety rules can create a negative environment for learning. It is possible to teach kids about dangerous topics without scaring them. After all, we manage to teach kids about the dangers of fire, traffic and other potential hazards. Safety training should be fun, and it can be when the right methods are used.

WHAT YOU CAN DO

❑ Set aside time at least once a month for safety training. Try to choose a time when the entire family can participate. Sunday afternoon or early evening is a good time for many families since things generally are winding down from the weekend and there is a lull before the coming week.

❑ Make a "lesson" plan of the skills you want your kids to learn and the activities you plan to use. Try to keep your plan as unstructured and informal as possible. The objective is to make learning fun and enjoyable so your kids will look forward to it, not dread it.

❑ Choose the kinds of activities that get everyone involved and hold kids' attention.

• Play acting is particularly good since it allows for plenty of participation and interaction.

• "What if" quiz games are good for introducing new concepts to kids, as are "Simon Says" and other repetitive type games.

• Fables and fantasies can be excellent teaching tools for young children. Using modern-day versions of classics and old standards is enjoyable for both parents and kids.

• Family viewing of certain television shows and animated videos with the right message is extremely effective, particularly when followed by a discussion of the values the show imparted.

SUPPLEMENTAL READING

For parents:

Creative Family Projects, Games & Activities, by Cynthia MacGregor

SAFETY BEGINS AT HOME

At the very least, children should expect to be safe and secure in the confines of their own home. Unfortunately, this isn't always the case. In fact, considering the number of cases of physical abuse, sexual abuse, child abductions, assaults and murders, the home can be a very dangerous place for many children. Addressing the social ills that lead to some of these crimes is well beyond the scope of this book. Unfortunately, there seem to be no effective protective measures for children at risk of being harmed by members of their immediate family. Usually, we don't learn of such risks until a child has been killed or injured by a family member. It's a very disturbing truth.

There are, however, a number of steps that responsible parents can take to protect their children from outsiders. Some of the steps entail making changes to the home itself, like fortifying doors and windows, installing security alarms and adding security lighting. But most involve making changes in habit patterns, then training our children to follow the examples we set. Unfortunately, when we're in familiar surroundings, we all have a tendency to lower our guard and become somewhat complacent. But the way things are today, complacency about crime can put your entire family in jeopardy.

14. Make Your Home More Secure.

A secure home is fundamental to the safety of every family member. A break-in or burglary at your home can have devastating effects on everyone in the household, but particularly on your kids. Their sense of well-being often is shattered when a crime is committed in what they perceive to be the safest of all places. Sometimes, the emotional scars from a break-in last for years in children, even if they are not at home at the time the incident occurs. Of course, should they be at home when a burglary is committed, they might be in extreme danger. Although the chances of this happening are slight, it is nonetheless a scenario that parents should anticipate and try to counter. Bear in mind that burglars almost always seek out the easiest target. By taking safety measures that make your home less vulnerable, you can reduce the risk of burglaries and crimes in the home.

WHAT YOU CAN DO

❑ Install an alarm system. Home security systems range in sophistication from a simple unit that sounds an alarm, to more elaborate systems linked to the police or security guards. Many security systems now are so reasonably priced that they cost about the same as monthly cable TV service. A reliable security system is well worth the money. The cost of a burglary could far outweigh the cost of an alarm system, particularly when you're talking about something as precious as your family. Also, some insurance companies offer a discount on home owner's insurance when you have an alarm system.

• If at all possible, choose an alarm system with a "panic button." This option enables you or your kids to alert police, fire or emergency service with the touch of a single button (see page 71).

• Another good feature to have is one that links your pager with your home security system. This option is particularly good if your kids must be home alone, since it enables you to remotely monitor their arrival and departure. You'll know the minute your kids come home, and the moment they happen to leave again.

• Other good options to consider: (1) a system that turns lights on and off following your daily routine to make it look like someone is at home while you are gone; (2) a system that enables you to turn on the lights and turn off the security system inside your house while you are still safely inside your car; (3) a system that allows you to remotely check and control your home security unit using a touchtone telephone.

• No matter which system you choose, you should place decals on your windows and a sign out front to warn burglars of its presence. The intent of alarms is to scare away intruders. If burglars know your home has an alarm, they might be deterred.

• Talk to friends and/or neighbors to get their recommendations about the most reliable security system.

❑ Strengthen and fortify all exterior doors and windows. Many intruders break in right through the door, either by unlocking it or kicking it in.

• All exterior doors should be hollow-core metal or solid-core wood and should fit snugly into the door frame.

• All exterior doors should swing inward, with the door hinges on the inside.

• Ideally, exterior doors should not have windows that a burglar can break and reach inside to unlock the door.

• Glass doors or doors with window panes should be equipped with a double-cylinder deadbolt lock. This type of lock requires a key to open the door either from the inside or outside, making it virtually impossible for a burglar to reach in and unlock the door. ***A word of caution:*** double-key deadbolts make it more difficult to get out of the house in case of a fire or other emergency. If you use such a lock, make sure the key is always handy for everyone in the house. *Make doubly sure that your kids always know where keys are located and how to unlock the door!*

• Do not rely on doorknob locks, night latches or chain locks. They are easily picked or pried open and offer almost no resistance to an intruder.

• Install deadbolt locks that extend a minimum of one inch into the door frame. You can strengthen the lock by adding a metal strike plate that extends into the studs around the door (most strike plates only extend into the molding around the door facing). Extending the plate into the stud makes it more difficult for a burglar to kick in the door.

• If you're unsure about locks, check with a reputable locksmith for recommendations on the best type of deadbolt lock for your doors. *Make sure your kids know how to lock and unlock any device you install! Never install a locking device that is too complicated or sophisticated for your kids to operate.* Otherwise, they could be trapped inside the house in case of an emergency.

• Brace exterior doors from the inside with a door wedge or rod-type device that further reduces the threat of "kick-burglars." Be sure to choose a device that can easily be opened from inside.

• Take care with house keys. Never hide them under a doormat, in the mailbox, etc. Burglars know all the best hiding places.

• Install a wide-angle peephole to enable you and your kids to see who is at the door. Make sure the peephole is placed low enough for kids to use. Teach your kids that they are never to open the door without first looking through the peephole to determine who is there. As a rule, you should never let young children answer the door (see page 68 for children who are at home alone). It's too easy for an intruder to trick a child into letting him into the house.

• If you have a pet door, make sure that it can be locked securely when you are gone. Some burglars can squeeze through these doors.

• If you have sliding patio doors, use a locking metal rod that prevents the door from being opened by an intruder. If that isn't feasible, place a piece of wood in the door channel. Additionally, to prevent sliding doors from being lifted out of the track, drill a hole in the middle of the frame where the doors overlap, and insert a pin, nail or lock into the hole.

• Install extra window locks, either a sash fastener that can be locked with a key or a key lock installed in the window bar. The ordinary sash fastener offers virtually no resistance at all to a burglar. Make sure the locking device can be opened easily from the inside in the event of a fire. *Be sure that your kids know where the keys are kept and how to lock and unlock these devices.*

• If you install burglar bars, make sure they are equipped with a locking device that enables them to be opened or removed from the inside. The wrong type of burglar bars can make your home a fire trap.

• Consider steel security shutters instead of burglar bars. Security shutters offer much the same protection as burglar bars. However, most security shutters can be opened easily from the inside, reducing the risk of someone being trapped by a fire or other emergency. *As is the case with all security devices, make sure your kids know how to operate them.*

❑ Consider getting a dog. Dogs have considerably better senses of hearing and smell, enabling them to detect the presence of intruders well in advance of humans. A dog's barking can alert you to danger, giving you time to take action beforehand. Also, it lets the intruder know that his presence has been detected. Many burglars will avoid a home where a loudly barking dog is present. Equally important, the right kind of dog can be an excellent companion for kids, especially those who are home alone.

• Check with a veterinarian or the police department for their recommendations on the best breed of dog for your situation. Generally a large dog offers better protection, but keep in mind that how loudly the dog barks is almost as important as the dog's size.

• A yard dog generally is a better deterrent, while a house dog offers better protection. Most dogs will not hesitate to attack an intruder, regardless of how large or intimidating the intruder might be.

• Before you decide on a dog, you should consider the nuisance factor. Dogs require care and nurturing, much like children. They can also be messy and destructive to landscaping and furnishings. Also, a dog that barks constantly will be of little use since you'll never know if it is barking at an intruder or simply barking at the moon. Such a dog is likely to alienate your neighbors and could possibly get you fined for disturbing the peace.

• Give a lot of thought to the breed you choose. Think long and hard before you purchase an attack dog or vicious breed. While these dogs do offer greater protection, they also pose a danger to young children in your household and other citizens in the neighborhood. *Never leave infants or young children alone with any large or vicious dog!*

• Thoroughly investigate any kennel before you buy a dog. There are some unscrupulous kennel owners who will sell you an inferior breed or poorly trained dog. A dog that has been improperly trained may be more vicious and unpredictable than a dog that has not been trained at all.

• If it's impractical for you to have a dog, consider purchasing a good quality "barking dog" alarm for your house. The better units sound like a vicious dog loudly barking inside the house. Some of these units can be set to go off if the doorbell rings or if someone tries to force entry into the house. While they may not fool every burglar, they might be a deterrent to some. You also can put up a "beware of dog" sign on your fence or in a window and leave a dog dish by the back door to further create the illusion that you have a dog inside.

❑ Make your home as visible as possible both night and day. Homes that are surrounded by high fences and shrubs are most inviting to thieves, day or night. And homes that are poorly lit give burglars the advantage of darkness.

- Ideally, shrubbery should be kept trimmed to no higher than three feet to help eliminate hiding places for criminals.

- Trees should be kept trimmed so that the bottom branches are no less than seven feet above the ground, and they should be trimmed back from windows and walls so they don't provide a convenient ladder.

- Keep your home's exterior well-lit at night. Use low-voltage landscape lighting to keep exterior walls illuminated. Install floodlights for your back yard, and leave your front porch light on.

- Leave a light on inside your garage at night, and keep the garage door locked.

- Leave a light on inside the house at night. If a burglar sees a light on, he can't be sure if somebody inside is awake, and this might make him think twice before trying to break in.

• If you live on a dark street, try to get together with other neighbors and petition the city for street lights.

• Visibility is particularly important if you live on or near a major thoroughfare. Burglars strike 40% more often within three blocks of a major thoroughfare that offers an easy escape route. And nearly 4 out of 10 residential burglaries occur at houses on corners.

❑ Keep lawn mowers, tools and bikes locked up at all times. Most residential burglaries are committed by petty thieves (often neighborhood teen-agers) who break into open garages.

❑ Don't let your kids leave their bicycles in the front yard or driveway without being locked. More than 15,000 bicycles are stolen every day in the U.S., and many are taken right from the front yard in broad daylight.

SUPPLEMENTAL READING

Don't Be the Next Victim. 50 Ways to Protect Yourself Against Crime, by Richard W. Eaves and Steven E. Watson

15. Teach Your Kids Home Safety Skills.

Providing adequate protection for kids in the home begins with basic safety skills. Most of these skills are based on common sense and are things many parents do as part of their routine. However, you can't assume that your kids learn these skills simply through observation. Like everything else, they must be taught by rote and repetition and be constantly reinforced.

The best way to teach these skills is through demonstration, or showing your kids first-hand exactly what to do. Then, use drills, exercises and other activities to reinforce their learning. This training should begin as soon as you feel your child is ready to learn, usually around the age of three or four.

WHAT YOU CAN DO

❑ Teach your kids to keep all doors and windows locked. Each time kids come into the house, they should lock the door behind them.

❑ Teach your kids how to use all locks and keys, as well as any security devices you have installed.

❑ Kids should know that they never open the door to a stranger. They should always look through the peephole to identify the person at the door. Your kids should be aware that most strangers who come to the door are there for legitimate reasons. But they also should know that the stranger at the door could be a burglar casing your home, or even worse. As a general rule, you should never let children under the age of eight or nine answer the door. Of course, children who are at home alone have no choice. You should give your children specific instructions about dealing with a person who comes to the door while they are home alone. Keep in mind that *your children should never ignore someone at the door.* If the person at the door happens to be a burglar and thinks no one is home, he might decide to break into the house. And that could put your children in great danger.

❑ When children are at home alone, they must be taught how to handle the various situations that might arise. There are almost certain to be times when someone comes to the door, and your child must know how to respond. For example, what does a child do if a salesman comes to the door? What about someone claiming to be a utility repairman? Or someone who asks to use the phone because of an emergency? The following guidelines might be useful in helping your child handle different situations. But regardless of the situation, *your child should always keep the door closed and locked any time there's a stranger at the door. Furthermore, your child should never give away the fact that he or she is at home alone.*

• If solicitors or sales people come to the door, your child should talk to them through the closed, locked door. Your child should never indicate that he or she is in the house alone. Instead, your child should say something like, "My dad can't come to the door now. Leave your card in the door and he will call you later if he's interested." (Using the term "Dad" may be stretching the truth in some cases, but as a rule, it is safer to indicate the presence of a male in the house.) Under no circumstances should your child open the door. It is helpful in this situation if you have a barking dog in the house to discourage someone with criminal intent. If you don't have a dog but you do have a good quality "barking dog" alarm (see page 64), your child should activate the alarm to give the impression that a dog is inside. Make sure your child knows how to use such an alarm.

• If a person comes to the door to make a delivery and insists that someone sign for it, your child should say something like, "My Dad can't come to the door right now. He wants you to leave the package by the front door, and he'll accept responsibility for it." If the person at the door persists, your child should say something like, "If you won't leave it by the door, my Dad said to bring it back tomorrow." Here again, it is helpful if you have a loudly barking dog inside. ***Note:*** Try to schedule any deliveries on dates you know an adult will be at home. Otherwise, arrange to have all packages delivered to your place of business or to a friend or neighbor. Try to avoid putting your children in the position of having to make decisions about opening the door to *any* stranger. In some cases, it might be worth getting a "shipping address" at a neighborhood postal box service.

• If a person comes to the door claiming to be from the police department, fire department, a utility company, etc., claiming that there is an emergency that requires evacuation of the house, your child should talk through the closed, locked door and say something like, "My Dad can't come to the door right now, but he's calling the company to verify the emergency. We will leave as soon as he confirms it." Then, your child should immediately call one of the parents, the block parent, PhoneFriend (see page 96) or some other designated adult for advice. If no one else is available, your child should call the company or organization the person at the door claims to represent to confirm the reason for the person being there. (Remember, phone numbers for the police department, fire department and utility companies should be available by the telephone at all times.) Unless your child can tell for sure that a real emergency exists (smells gas or smoke, sees flames or electrical sparks, etc.) he or she should not open the door before getting confirmation.

• Should the person at the door become belligerent or refuse to leave, your child should call the police at once on the regular police line, explain the situation and ask that a patrol car be sent. If the person at the door attempts to force entry, your child should try to get out of the house immediately and run to a neighbor's or other safe place and dial 911. If your child is unable to get out of the house, he or she should quickly call 911, then try to get into a room with a door that can be closed and locked from inside (see page 109). If you have an alarm system with a "panic button," the child should activate it once he or she is inside the locked room. Remember, dialing 911 probably will get a faster response than a panic button, so teach your kids to call 911 if there's time before retreating to another room. Hopefully, your child will never be faced with such a situation, but it is imperative that he or she be prepared in the event it ever occurs.

❑ Teach your kids proper phone safety. This is important for all children, but vital for those who are home alone.

- When your children answer the phone, they should never give information to strangers regarding who is and isn't home or how long anyone is expected to be gone. *They should never tell the caller that they are home alone.* It is best to give the impression that a parent, preferably the father, is at home but unavailable to come to the phone. Instruct your child to tell the caller to leave a number and the parent will call back (see the discussion of cordless phones and hold buttons on page 109). Remember, it is not a good idea to let the phone go unanswered, since it might give the impression that no one is at home. If the caller is a burglar casing houses, he might come right over. If you absolutely do not want children to answer the phone when you're gone, purchase an answering machine. However, never leave a message that says you're not at home. Instead, have the message give the impression that you're in the house but unable to come to the phone, something like, "We're unable to take your call right now, but we'll get back to you as soon as possible." It's a good idea to use a male voice when recording messages, whether or not there is actually a male in the household.

• When children answer the phone to an obscene caller, they should hang up the phone immediately. *They should not respond at all.* And they should try not to cry or show their fear. This may be the response the caller is trying to elicit. If the caller continues to call back, the child should contact a parent or pre-designated adult for assistance. If the child keeps answering, the caller may suspect the child is home alone. Make sure your child knows to report any obscene phone calls to you. You should immediately call the police and report the incident. Additionally, if you receive an abnormal number of wrong numbers, hang-ups or nuisance calls, you should notify the police, since the calls might be a burglar casing houses. Your local phone company can also provide assistance in helping block or eliminate obscene or harassing phone calls (see page 101).

• Consider getting an unlisted phone number. This is especially helpful if your kids have to be at home alone. An unlisted phone number gives you more control over who calls your home and who doesn't.

SUPPLEMENTAL READING

The Safe Child Book, by Sherryll Kerns Kraizer

16. Get Involved with Your Neighborhood Watch Program.

One of the best ways to protect children is to band with other citizens in a collective and cooperative effort to keep your neighborhood safe. These neighborhood watch programs are relatively easy to get started, and they have proved to be very effective in reducing burglaries, drug dealing and other crimes that impact neighborhoods. At the very least, such programs contribute to neighborhood cohesiveness and unity, and this by itself can have a positive effect on safety.

Some programs consist of residents of a single block, while others encompass a broader area, usually the entire neighborhood. In either case, citizens are trained by law enforcement officials to watch for and report criminal or suspicious activities in their neighborhood.

In high-crime areas, citizens actually patrol the streets themselves (or hire security companies to provide patrols). These citizen patrols usually are equipped with CB radios or walkie-talkies to communicate with a resident volunteer dispatcher. In some cases, the police even provide special radio frequencies or emergency phone numbers. The Crime Prevention Division of your police department can give you more details.

WHAT YOU CAN DO

❑ If there's a neighborhood watch program where you live, get involved. The more active the residents are, the better the program will work. By making it more difficult for criminals to operate in your neighborhood, you'll be creating a safer environment for all the children who live there.

❑ Don't wait for crime to become a problem in your neighborhood. If there's not a crime watch program available, get one started today. If necessary, start small, possibly with residents only on your block. Begin by talking to the neighbors immediately adjacent to your home. You will find that most neighbors share your concern and are willing to cooperate. Call your local police or sheriff's department for more information about setting up and maintaining the program. The police in almost every city are eager for citizen participation in crime prevention programs such as these.

❑ Make a diagram of your block with the name, address and phone number of each resident. If you observe suspicious activity, call and alert your neighbor. It may turn out to be totally innocent, in which case your neighbor will know what's going on. If your neighbor isn't home, you should call the police and report any suspicious activity you observe. Unless you perceive it to be an emergency, however, do not use the 911 number (the 911 number must be kept open for genuine emergencies). Call the police on the regular line instead. *Never try to intervene yourself. Wait for the police to arrive.*

❑ Remember, protecting children against crime can best be accomplished by you and your neighbors. The police can do little until after a crime takes place. By joining with your neighbors in a concerted effort, you have the most power to prevent crimes where you live.

17. Keep a Close Eye on Your Kids While They're Playing in the Yard.

At one time, parents felt their kids were safe when they were playing in the neighborhood. That feeling has changed greatly in recent years. Nowadays, parents can't even feel safe when their kids are playing in their own yard. There have been too many cases of a child being taken from the yard while one of the parents was inside working or cleaning the house.

WHAT YOU CAN DO

❑ Don't allow your child to play alone in the front yard. And don't lower your guard just because your child seems to be secure in a fenced-in back yard. Young children, even infants in playpens, have disappeared from their back yard when a parent stepped inside the house for just a minute.

❑ If at all possible, try to time your yard work to coincide with play time so you can be outside with your child.

❑ If you can't be outside with your kids, try to do work inside the house that enables you to keep your child in view at all times.

❑ If you can't keep your child in view, check on him or her at least every five minutes. Better yet, try to find inside activities for your child until you can go outside together.

❑ If you can possibly afford one, it's a good idea to have some type of remote surveillance/observation equipment to monitor your children when you can't keep them in view. For less than $100, you can purchase a walkie-talkie type system that allows you to listen to your children's activities while they're playing outside. The child has a transmitter and you have the receiver. A more elaborate system allows you to visually monitor your children, whether they are inside the home or in the back yard. It's called the Baby Cam or Nanny Cam, and it can be purchased for under $400. It allows you to see and hear your kids via a camera with an audio pick-up that transmits through your home's electrical system to a small video monitor.

❑ Keep your fence gate locked at all times.

❑ Attach a bell or other noise-maker to the gate so that you'll know if the gate is being opened.

❑ Make sure your child knows the rules regarding leaving the yard or talking to any strangers that happen by (see page 44).

18. Never Assume That Your Neighborhood Is Completely Safe.

Most neighborhoods today aren't like they used to be. Neighborhoods were once very safe havens for children, mainly because the residents would watch out for their neighbors, as well as neighborhood kids. Children knew that they could turn to their neighbors for help if they ever needed it.

The mobility of our society today has contributed greatly to the disintegration of neighborhood unity. Now, it's not uncommon for neighbors to remain virtual strangers, knowing each other only by sight. Gone is that neighborhood unity and the informal network of adults who watched out for the welfare of the kids who lived on the block. A return to that kind of safety system would greatly diminish the chances of your child's becoming a victim of crime. It is needed today more than ever.

Much of the crime that has plagued residents of the inner city now has spread to suburban and rural areas. The neighborhood where you live might have been very safe and secure at one time. But like all things, it probably has changed, and not necessarily for the better. In today's world, there simply is no such place as a totally secure neighborhood. Even the newer residential areas, complete with moats, fences, and security guards, are vulnerable. It's unfortunate, but when it comes to the safety of your children, you must prepare them for worst-case scenarios. And that includes being on the alert even in the familiar confines of their own neighborhood, regardless of how safe it may seem to be.

WHAT YOU CAN DO

❑ Make it a rule for your kids to get your permission before they leave your yard or go to a friend's home to play. Check with their friend's parents to make sure someone will be there to watch the kids.

❑ Set a time for your kids to return home. If they are delayed for any reason, they should call and let you know.

❑ Supervise your kids as much as possible while they are playing in the neighborhood.

❑ Encourage your kids to play in groups, out in the open where you can keep them in sight.

❑ Have your kids go to the bus stop in a group. If there are no other kids on the block who ride their bus, walk your child to and from the stop.

❑ Walk the neighborhood with your kids and point out any places you think they should avoid. Draw them a neighborhood safety map that includes the safest route to the homes of various friends, the bus stop, the store, etc.

❑ Watch for signs of gang activity in your neighborhood. Graffiti and vandalism are usually the first signs. Some communities have found that removing graffiti immediately helps impede the spread of gang activity. Contact your local police or sheriff's department. They usually have a gang task force that can offer additional information, or in some cases, provide extra patrol units to head off potential problems. It is very important for residents to take immediate action upon observing signs of gang activity. The objective is to keep it from growing and spreading throughout your neighborhood.

❑ Try to keep abandoned cars off the streets in and around your neighborhood. In addition to being eyesores, they can be hazardous for kids to be around. Sometimes they're used by transients and/or drug dealers and addicts. They are also tempting targets of vandals. Once vandalism gets started, it can quickly spread and contribute to gang activity and the general decline of a neighborhood. Call the police or sheriff's department to report abandoned vehicles.

❑ Try to keep your neighborhood free of abandoned houses and buildings. These areas are often used by drug dealers and transients and generally contribute to the decline of a neighborhood. Call your city's zoning or planning commission to determine what can be done about abandoned buildings.

❑ Keep vacant lots clean and mowed. Do not let weeds grow up and trash accumulate. Not only does this create a blight on your neighborhood, it can also attract vagrants and/or foster criminal activities. It also creates another hazardous area for children. As in the case of abandoned buildings, contact the zoning or planning commission in your city. If you don't get action, contact the owner of the lot and insist that it be kept clean. In some cases, individual neighbors might be able to sue the land owner for creating a public nuisance. Of course, this can be a lengthy process. In the interim, organize a clean-up day and clear the lot of trash and debris.

❑ Be wary of any strangers who appear in the neighborhood, even those who appear to be solicitors or salesmen.

❑ Get to know your neighbors, especially those on both sides and across the street from your home.

❑ Get involved in your neighborhood watch program (see page 74). Police statistics show that in neighborhoods where such programs are used, crime is substantially reduced. Your local law enforcement agency can help you get the program started.

❑ If you live in a neighborhood with a severe crime problem, consider establishing a "Citizens on Patrol" program. This system makes use of resident volunteers who patrol the neighborhood around the clock to keep an eye out for criminal activities and report them to police. Here again, the police or sheriff's department can help you get the program established in your neighborhood.

❑ Try to establish a "Block Parent" program for your street. A Block Parent is a responsible adult who agrees to assist children who come to the door in need of help. The Block Parent is a short-term, temporary guardian who cares for the child until the parent or police arrive. *A Block Parent is not a babysitter or substitute for parental responsibility.*

19. Carefully Screen Baby-sitters, Maids and Other Help.

At one time or another, most parents have to leave their kids with a baby-sitter. Sometimes it's a friend or relative. Other times, it may be a complete stranger. Either way, it is very important to evaluate anyone with whom you entrust your children.

Typically, most baby-sitters are teenagers from the neighborhood. As nice and trustworthy as they may seem, they could pose a security problem for your children. You may have known the teen down the block for years, even her family. But what about her friends? What if she has a boyfriend on drugs who comes to visit her while she is baby-sitting with your kids? You certainly don't want to expose your kids to such a person. You can never take anything for granted when it comes to the safety of your children. Most of the time, baby-sitters are people you don't know well at all.

Since most child molesters are men, you should be cautious about leaving children with a male, even if he is a relative. Uncles and cousins have been known to molest young nephews and cousins. Of course, your knowledge of the relative should be the determining factor. In most cases, a male relative will pose no sexual threat to children, but it is still important for you to be aware that such cases have occurred in the past. And the use of a male non-relative might increase the chances of your child being molested. This certainly isn't meant to cast doubt upon all males, but the fact remains that most child molestation is committed by men.

WHAT YOU CAN DO

❑ Never let anyone look after your kids or work in your home until you have thoroughly checked out the person.

❑ Get references from everyone you employ in your home, from the occasional baby-sitter to a live-in maid. Never employ a person who can't or won't supply references.

❑ Check all references thoroughly. If there is the slightest doubt about the person, you probably should find someone else.

❑ If you have any reservations at all about live-in domestic help, it may be advisable to have a background investigation conducted by a reputable investigative agency.

❑ Be sure to check the references of any domestic employment agencies you use. Their people are probably only as good as the agency itself.

❑ When domestic help leaves your employ, it's advisable to change the locks on all exterior doors.

❑ Temporary workers in your home (painters, carpenters, etc.) may pose a particular threat to your children, since it's almost impossible to check out each individual a construction contractor may hire. Try to deal only with reputable contractors who provide a surety bond for each employee and/or subcontractor who will be working in your home. Never leave children alone in the house while temporary workers are there.

❑ Try to hire well-qualified sitters, preferably limited to individuals who have completed a course in baby-sitting. Such courses usually cover information on all facets of temporary care for kids, from infants to pre-teens.

❑ When hiring a baby-sitter, spell out the rules beforehand. If you're not sure the sitter will strictly follow your instructions, try to find someone else.

❑ Give the baby-sitter clear and complete written instructions, including where you will be and the phone number where you can be reached. Make sure you include the name and number of a relative or neighbor to contact in case of an emergency, the name of your family doctor, medications (if any) that must be administered, and phone numbers for the police, fire department and ambulance service.

❑ It's never a good idea to allow a baby-sitter to have friends over. While you have checked out the sitter, you know nothing at all about his/her friends. Even a trustworthy friend of the baby-sitter might be enough of a distraction to cause him/her to be less attentive to your child.

20. Exercise Extreme Care If You Have Guns in Your Home.

There are more than 200 million firearms in circulation in America today, and more than half of all households have at least one gun. Regardless of how you feel about having guns in your home, there are a few facts you should know.

- Guns in the home are 40 times more likely to be used against another family member, a relative or an acquaintance than against an intruder.

- A child dies from gunshot wounds every two hours in the United States.

- Every day, more than a million "latchkey" kids are alone in a home where there's a gun.

- Kids as young as six have brought guns to school. It is estimated that 80% to 90% of kids who brought guns to school took the weapons from their homes.

- The number of young people 17 and under who were arrested for murder increased 60% nationwide between 1981 and 1990. Handguns are the weapons used in seven of every ten murders committed in the U.S.

If you exercise your right to keep guns in your home, you also must take responsibility for the safe use and storage of those weapons. If you have kids and guns in your home, one moment of laxity, one slight mistake, is all it takes for tragedy to strike.

WHAT YOU CAN DO

❑ Never keep a loaded gun in your home! With kids around, this is a disaster waiting to happen.

❑ Keep guns locked and unloaded. Special trigger locks should be kept on every gun in the house.

❑ Keep all firearms in a sturdy gun safe that is kept locked at all times. Keep the key in a secure place where you are certain children cannot find it.

❑ Store guns and ammunition separately. Even if you keep the gun locked, there's always the chance it could discharge accidentally if a child happened to load it. Ammunition should be kept under lock and key at all times.

❑ If you decide to purchase a handgun for protection, buy only the best. And buy from a reputable arms dealer. Cheap handguns like those often sold at gun shows have been known to explode when discharged. Sometimes they discharge without the trigger being pulled. Furthermore, they are less likely to be accurate.

❑ It's very important that you receive the proper training in the care and use of any firearm you have.

❑ It's equally important that you teach your kids about the dangers of guns. Explain to kids why you have a gun in your home. Continually reinforce the rule that they are never to play with guns or ammunition. There should be a firm rule that your kids never remove a gun or ammunition from the storage safe.

❑ Bear in mind that a gun you purchase for defense can just as easily be used against you or a member of your family.

WHEN KIDS ARE HOME ALONE

Leaving kids at home alone should be a last resort for any parent. In some states, it is against the law if a child is under the age of 12. Beyond that, however, there simply are too many potential perils to make such a decision lightly.

If there is any alternative such as day-care, after-school care or a responsible friend or relative, we urge you to consider it. Also, with the growing trend of companies allowing employees to "telecommute" and work at home, some parents now have options that weren't available a few years ago. Check with your employer about such an arrangement.

Before leaving children alone at home, parents must first determine whether the children are ready for such responsibility. Their age as well as their maturity has to be considered. In addition to being able to lock and unlock doors, operate home security devices and, in some cases, prepare meals, a child must be able to cope with fear, loneliness, boredom and potential emergencies. Once it has been determined to leave children at home alone, parents must teach their kids how to cope with every eventuality. *Nothing can be left to chance!*

The ideal situation would be to have a "block parent" (see page 83) who could provide temporary assistance or shelter if there's an emergency which the child does not know how to handle. The next best thing would be to have a PhoneFriend (see page 96) the child can call in the event the parents can't be reached. It's important that there be an adult available, either yourself, your spouse, a relative or friend, when your child is faced with an unforeseen problem or emergency.

21. Set and Enforce Rules for Your Kids to Follow.

It's extremely important that your kids know exactly what they can and cannot do when they are home alone. If they are pre-teens, you might want them to stay inside the house and not allow friends over. If they are responsible teens, you might allow them more freedom, provided they have your permission. Remember, it's not enough to merely tell your kids the do's and don'ts. The rules must be set by you, then rehearsed over and over with your kids.

When laying out rules, try to state them in positive terms. Rules that begin with "don't" can make children resentful and rebellious, especially if they are adolescents. Instead, spell out rules with phrases like, "when you get home, be sure to..."

Never assume that all rules will be obeyed. Even the best of kids will occasionally break the rules. Establish consequences for following rules. This involves not only punishment for breaking rules but also rewards for sticking to them. Parents should be able to check each day to make sure rules are being followed.

If you have a close, trusted friend or neighbor, ask that person to help you check and report any serious violations. Make sure your kids know that you have asked the neighbor's help, so it won't appear that your neighbor is being nosy. Remember, though, it's not your friend's or neighbor's job to see that your rules are followed. That is strictly a parental responsibility.

WHAT YOU CAN DO

❑ Put all rules in writing, and post them in a prominent place in the house.

❑ Go over the rules with your kids from time to time to make sure they fully understand them.

❑ Try to be fair about the rules you set, but don't be overly lenient. It is much better to be cautious about something as serious as your child's safety.

❑ Stick to your rules consistently. Don't allow exceptions to any rule unless your child has your permission beforehand. Do not make a habit of bending the rules.

❑ Rewarding your kids for following the rules generally will be more effective than punishing them for breaking rules.

❑ Never assume that any child will follow all the rules all the time. If possible, try to have a trusted friend or relative look in on the kids from time to time to be sure that rules are being followed.

❑ Occasionally, try to come home early to see whether rules are being obeyed. Let your kids know that your actions are part of the plan for their safety and are not meant to indicate your distrust.

22. Make Sure Your Kids Know How and Whom to Call for Help.

It isn't enough merely to post emergency numbers by the phone and expect kids to know how to use them. Children must be trained to know precisely how and under what circumstances they are to use emergency numbers. For example, 911 is the number to call when there is a serious emergency. It will get a response from the police, the fire department or ambulance service. But do your kids know what constitutes an emergency? What if they hear a noise in the house? Do they call 911 or do they call the police on the regular line? Each situation must be clearly defined for your kids.

You should try to be available by phone at all times throughout the day. In addition, you should try to have another responsible adult available (a close neighbor, trusted friend or relative) for your kids to call in the event they are unable to reach you by phone. In some communities, kids have their own special "phone friend."

PhoneFriend is a number kids can call just to have someone to talk to, whether they simply are lonely, scared or have a situation they don't know how to handle. This service was established several years ago by the American Association of University Women (AAUW) exclusively for children who are home alone. Check the phone book to see if there is a PhoneFriend program in your area. If you find a PhoneFriend, include the number on the child's phone list. Remember, however, *a PhoneFriend is not meant to be a substitute for parental supervision.*

WHAT YOU CAN DO

❑ Keep emergency numbers by the phone at all times.

❑ Do not assume that your kids automatically know how to dial different numbers or how to use all telephone equipment. Nowadays, there are many different types of phone equipment, and they're not all as simple to operate as lifting the receiver and entering numbers on the touchtone. It's a good idea to show your kids how to use various types of phones, including pay phones.

❑ If at all possible, purchase a telephone with speed dialing and/or pre-programmed, one-number dialing. With this type of telephone, your child can call a number by depressing a single button. Try to limit the programmed numbers to two or three of the most important numbers (your work number, PhoneFriend, etc.). Make sure your child commits the programmed numbers to memory. As a back-up, keep the programmed numbers by the phone at all times.

❑ Run through drills with your kids that cover different situations. Explain exactly which number your child should call for each situation. Your child should know to immediately call 911 in a serious emergency. Make sure your child fully understands what constitutes an emergency.

❑ When calling an emergency number, kids must be taught the importance of speaking as clearly as possible. They should first give their address; second, they should explain the emergency; third, they should tell the dispatcher that they are a child at home alone. They should then follow the instructions given by the dispatcher (usually, to stay on the phone or try to get out of the house) or answer any questions the dispatcher might ask.

❑ Your kids should know that in some emergencies such as a fire or an attempted burglary or break-in, their first course of action should be to get out of the house immediately and go to a neighboring home or other safe place to summon help. Make sure your kids know the best escape route from each room in the house.

❑ In areas that do not have 911 service, teach your kids that they can dial "0" and get a telephone operator who usually can summon emergency help.

❑ Make sure your kids know how to reach you by phone at all times of the day. If you leave your office for an appointment at another location, get the number and leave it with your company's receptionist, or leave a message on your answering machine at home. Don't forget to explain to your kids that they are sometimes put on hold when they call a business number.

❑ If you can possibly afford an answering machine or answering service, get one. This will allow you to leave messages for your kids whenever plans change. Check with your local telephone company. Most phone companies offer voice mail services for a small monthly fee.

❑ If you have a beeper or cellular phone, make sure that your kids have the number so they can contact you at any time during the day. Even if they have a phone friend, there are sure to be situations to arise that only the parents can handle.

❑ Always try to have a phone friend for your kids to call when they can't get in touch with you. Make sure they know the number. Most importantly, *make sure your kids understand that in a serious emergency, they should immediately dial 911, not the phone friend. In an emergency, every second is crucial.*

ADVANCED TELEPHONE SAFETY INFORMATION

The telephone has long played an important role in keeping kids safe. And with continuing advances in technology, its role is growing. Today, numerous options are available in most areas to assist in educating children about proper telephone usage, phone etiquette and phone safety. To help you determine which options are best for your particular situation, the following is a summary of available services to consider. Contact your local phone company for rates and availability in your area.

Voice Dialing and Speed Dialing

Voice Dialing is especially helpful for small children who may have trouble dialing a phone. With Voice Dial, a child need only say, "Call Mom," or "Grandpa's House," and the call will be placed to the phone number programmed to respond to that particular voice command. As with all important numbers, Voice Dial commands and numbers should also be kept by the telephone for easy reference. ***Note:*** Because stress can alter voice patterns, children should be taught to always dial 911 in an emergency and not rely on Voice Dial.

If Voice Dialing is not available in your area, consider subscribing to Speed Dialing. With Speed Dialing, only two or three buttons need to be pressed for a programmed number to complete a call.

Many telephone sets are also equipped with speed dialing buttons, in which case only one button need be pressed. If you have very young children, you might consider taping a small photo of the person who will receive the call (Mom, Dad, Grandma, etc.) next to the speed dialing button. That will clearly identify the speed dialing button and the person whom the call will reach.

Bear in mind, however, that children still need to learn how to dial the phone. Voice Dialing and

Speed Dialing will only work on phone numbers or telephone equipment where they are programmed to work. Pay phones, school phones and neighbors' phones will not respond to your child's voice commands or the Speed Dialing command of your home phone.

In some areas, local phone numbers may be prefaced with more than one area code. If your telephone service area consists of multiple area codes, your children should be taught to dial all ten digits to ensure local calls will be completed. Check with your local telephone company for complete dialing insructions in your area.

Caller ID, Priority Call and Personalized Ring

A Caller ID unit by the telephone gives children valuable information, as well as a feeling of control and security. With Caller ID, children can be taught to answer the phone only when certain numbers or names appear on the box, such as those of parents or grandparents. If a name or number appears on the Caller ID box that your child does not recognize, instruct your child to let your answering machine or voice mail pick up the call.

If your Caller ID has a memory feature, instruct children not to delete names or numbers until you have been able to review them. Many obscene or threatening callers choose to block their numbers, which means their number does not show up on Caller ID. You can respond to such calls with Anonymous Call Rejection service which prevents blocked calls from being received and informs the caller that your home does not accept anonymous calls.

To stop repeat harassing or threatening calls, you can use Call Blocker service. By programming to block the last call or a specific telephone number, your phone will not ring when called by these numbers, and the caller will be informed that you are not accepting calls at this time.

If Caller ID is not available in your area, consider Priority Call or Personalized Ring.

With Priority Call, you can assign a special ring to certain incoming telephone numbers, like your work number, grandparents or a neighborhood friend. Your children can be instructed to answer the phone only when they hear the special ring of a Priority Call, but not when they hear a regular ring.

With Personalized Ring, your children can have their own phone number, which is answered on your regular line. Children can be instructed not to answer any calls except those to their number, which is indicated by a distinctive Personalized Ring. This allows your children to answer those calls specifically for them.

Additional Telephone Safety Tips

❑ If your family is threatened by a caller, contact your local telephone company to activate Call Trace. Many times, the call trace report will be sent to your local police department, so you must be prepared to take legal action against the caller.

❑ A cellular phone may be the best defense in crises. Older children should understand that a cellular phone will work even if the line to the regular phone is out or they are forced to get out of the house in an emergency.

❑ Children should carry a small list of important phone numbers at all times to use when away from home. If the child is too young to carry a wallet or purse, the list could be laminated and tucked inside one of their shoes.

❑ It's also a good idea for kids to carry a prepaid calling card to enable them to reach you by pay phone whenever necessary. A prepaid calling card will relieve your kids of the temptation to spend change they have been given for pay phones.

❑ When children visit nearby friends, neighbors or family members, consider Call Forwarding service to forward your call and other important calls to your child away from home.

❑ Children at home alone should be taught not to use speaker phones. Background noises may reveal the absence of an adult.

❑ Children should be instructed never to play "phone games," like continuously returning the last call received, or placing prank calls. Adults may threaten children who do this, as well as bring legal action against the kids' parents.

❑ As children spend more time on the phone, it becomes increasingly difficult to reach them. If that's the case in your household, you might consider Call-Waiting service. When you need to reach your child and the child is on another call, Call-Waiting alerts your child to an incoming call. Children should be taught how to depress the switchhook or use the flash button to take the new call.

❑ Because of the variety of telephone equipment available, children should be taught how to depress the switchhook and how to properly hang up all the phones in your household. Portable phones can be particularly confusing to small children, and a phone off-the-hook disables the calling capability of the entire household.

❑ Children should be taught not to take telephones into water (bathtubs, pools, etc.) because of the danger of electrocution.

❑ Finally, if your child uses a computer and modem, consider getting a separate phone line for the computer, leaving the main phone line free for telephone calls. Advanced calling features of your telephone equipment may not work when the phone line is being used by a computer.

23. Stay in Touch with Your Kids throughout the Day.

Nothing is more reassuring to a child who's home alone than the voice of Mom or Dad. And reassurance is one thing such a child definitely needs, even a cocky teenager. Equally important, contact with your kids might help head off problems or unsafe situations before they develop. It also gives you, to some degree, an indication of how well rules are being followed.

If at all possible, there should be a standing rule that kids call you and check in the moment they get home from school. This lets you know that your kids have reached home safely and that everything is okay in the household. You can use this call to reinforce some of the safety rules.

You should try to call back later in the day to confirm that everything is still okay. It's best to have a pre-determined time for this call so your kids will be expecting it. Make sure your kids know the rules regarding safe use of the telephone (see page 71).

If you have a rule that kids are not to answer the phone while you're away, establish some sort of ring code so they'll know it's you calling (two rings and a hang-up then call back, etc.). Even better, check with your local phone company about such services as Caller ID, Priority Call or Personalized Ring (see page 101). Another option is to provide your child with a beeper and simply page your child for a call-back. (If you decide on a beeper, check with your school to determine if it's acceptable for the child to bring it to class. Some school districts prohibit beepers since they are often used by drug dealers.)

If your job situation permits it, you should also make a habit of calling your kids at random times during the day. The frequency of these calls will be determined by the age and/or maturity of your child, and the situation at home. Here again, use some sort of code in cases where answering the phone is prohibited. Or leave a message on your answering machine or service asking for an immediate call back.

WHAT YOU CAN DO

❑ Set pre-determined times for your kids to call you and check in throughout the day. Calling when they come home from school, play or visits with friends should be mandatory.

❑ If your work environment does not allow you to receive phone calls, try to arrange for a relative or neighbor to take the call. *It's extremely important that a responsible adult know that the child has arrived home safely.*

❑ Try to have pre-determined times that you call home to check on your kids.

❑ If at all possible, call home at random times throughout the day to check on your kids. Establish some sort of ring code so your kids will know you are the person calling. Even better, check with your phone company to see if they offer services like Caller ID, Priority Call or Personalized Ring.

❑ If you can afford a beeper or cellular phone, try to have one or the other with you at all times. These communication tools can be a tremendous help in maintaining contact with your kids. Make sure your kids know your cellular phone or beeper number.

24. Have an Emergency Plan in Place.

When children come home to an empty house, they should already have instructions on how to handle situations that are out of the ordinary. For instance, if something looks suspicious, like an open door or broken window, the child should know not to go inside. Instead, the child should go to a trusted neighbor's or to the nearest phone in a safe place and call to determine whether another family member has come home early.

No matter how well you plan, there are bound to be times when your kids will have to face uncertain situations. They may even have to contend with a full-blown emergency. And if that ever occurs, they must know exactly what to do.

WHAT YOU CAN DO

❑ Always have a responsible adult your children can turn to in the event of an emergency (a neighbor, a relative, a phone friend or a block parent).

❑ Try to plan for every eventuality, no matter how remote it may seem. Rehearse different situations, and drill your kids on the appropriate course of action. Do not leave anything to the imagination. Be clear and precise. If your kids have been taught what to do, they will be less likely to panic in the face of a real emergency.

❑ Help your kids memorize emergency phone numbers. In a critical situation, they may not have time to stop and look up a number, even if it's right by the telephone.

❑ Make sure your kids know emergency escape routes from each room in your home. Periodically conduct fire drills and/or "escape" drills.

❑ If possible, try to create a "safe room" where your kids could retreat in the event they feel threatened. Ideally, this room will have a hollow-core metal or solid-core wood door with a one-inch deadbolt that locks from the inside. It also will have a telephone and/or a "panic button" tied to a home security system, plus a small outside window that provides an avenue of escape. A bathroom, bedroom or large closet can be made into a "safe room" without a great deal of expense.

❑ Purchase a cordless telephone, preferably one with a "hold" button, and teach your kids how to use it. With a cordless phone, your child can call for help and stay on the line even if he or she has to retreat to a "safe room" or to another room in the house. A "hold" button enables your child to "buy some time" to compose himself/herself when in doubt about how to handle a call. Also, if your telephone is equipped for two lines and you have a second phone line, your child can call you on one line while the caller is on hold on the other line. Try to include Speed Dialing or Voice Dialing in the telephone service you select (see page 100).

SUPPLEMENTAL READING

For kids:

The Official Kids' Survival Kit. How to Do Things on Your Own, by E. Chabah and P. Fortunato

Alone at Home. A Kid's Guide to Being in Charge, by Ann Banks

For parents:

Home Alone Kids. The Working Parents' Guide to Providing the Best Care for a Child, by Bryand Robinson

Family Rules. Raising Responsible Children Without Yelling or Nagging, by Kenneth Kaye

ADDITIONAL INFORMATION

For parents and kids:

The video *Home Alone: A Kid's Guide,* featuring Malcolm-Jamal Warner (of The Bill Cosby Show) and young friends, demonstrates ways to increase the safety of kids who are home alone. Try to watch this community service video with your kids. It can be checked out free of charge at Blockbuster Video stores.

WHEN YOUR KIDS GO TO SCHOOL

School safety has become one of the most important issues of the day for both parents and educators. Much of their concern springs from the terrible tragedies that have occurred recently at various schools across America and the fear that a copycat might attempt a repeat.

Many school systems have implemented advanced security systems and procedures to enhance the safety of students and faculty. In some schools, security cameras monitor hallways and classrooms; exterior cameras and perimeter fences help secure the grounds; everyone who comes on campus must wear an identification badge at all times; metal detectors, drug-sniffing dogs and random drug checks are part of the regimen. Some schools have gone so far as to hire armed security guards to patrol the hallways and grounds.

Ironically, statistics show that school violence is actually on the decline in America. U.S. Department of Justice figures indicate that there were about half the number of school-related violent deaths in 1998 than in 1992. And a study by the *Journal of the American Medical Association* showed a 30% decrease in school violence between 1991 and 1997.

Experts attribute this decline to heightened school security and to the increased involvement of concerned parents. As with everything in the lives of children, parental participation and oversight are the best security measures of all.

25. Participate in Your Kids' School Lives.

Active involvement in your children's school lives is important not only for their education, but also for their safety and well-being. Getting involved entails more than just showing up for the school play. It requires making regular visits to the school, meeting with teachers and counselors and joining forces with other parents to help establish and implement certain school policies. *As a rule, the schools with the most parental involvement provide the best education and the safest environment.*

WHAT YOU CAN DO

❑ Try to visit your child's school at least once a month. This not only will help you track your child's educational progress, but also will keep you abreast of any safety problems that may arise.

❑ Make random visits from time to time. As a parent, you have the right to observe your child in the classroom so long as you check in with the front office before proceeding to the classroom.

❑ Learn your children's schedules. You should know what time they are to arrive each morning and what time they leave. If they ride the bus, know what time they get on and off the bus, as well as the time it takes to get to and from the bus stop. If they walk or ride a bike to school, know how long it takes and the route they follow. Do not allow them to take any route that might be dangerous. If need be, drive them to school or establish a car pool with other parents.

❑ If your children participate in extra-curricular activities such as sports, band, debate, etc., make sure you know the schedule for these activities as well as the level of adult supervision.

❑ Discourage your kids from going early or staying late unless there is adult supervision. There are simply too many things that can go wrong when activities are unsupervised, especially when you consider the prevalence of guns, drugs and gang activities in and around many schools. The safest course of action is to have your kids go straight to school and return home at the normal time unless they are engaged in school-sanctioned activities. Of course, all after-school activities should be well supervised.

❑ Never give a blanket approval for your kids to be taken from school on field trips. You have a right to know where your kids are going and for what reason each time they leave school. If you deny your approval for your child to leave school, find out from the school what arrangements will be made for your child. If you feel the arrangements don't provide adequate supervision and security for your child, it's probably safest for you to make other plans.

❑ Try to volunteer as much of your time as possible to act as chaperone when your children go on field trips or overnight excursions.

❑ Learn the dress code for your school and encourage your children to follow it (see page 116).

❑ Make sure you know all the rules and regulations that govern what your children can and cannot bring to school. For example, many schools have banned beepers and cellular telephones since these are often used by drug dealers. Other schools have banned such things as backpacks and school bags since they are sometimes used for carrying concealed weapons.

❑ Get involved with your school's parent-teacher organization. Working within such groups is one of the best ways to effect any changes that need to be made in either the school's curriculum or safety procedures.

❑ If your child attends a school that has a high crime rate, join with parents, the police and school officials to establish a school safety task force. Such groups in various cities have helped reduce criminal activity in and around schools by serving as auxiliary hall patrols, lunchroom and playground monitors, street crossing guards, neighborhood patrols and block parents. Without question, *the presence of responsible parents in and around schools is one of the best crime deterrents of all!*

❑ Make sure your school has a policy of notifying you when your child is absent from school. Many school districts routinely call the home early in the day when the child is absent. This is an important tool for protecting your children since it can provide early warning if a child is missing or has had an accident while on the way to school. To ensure that the program works efficiently, *it is incumbent upon each parent to notify the school on the days their child will be absent.* It's also imperative that parents provide the school with current phone numbers (home, business, etc.) where they can be reached when the school is inquiring about an unexplained absence.

26. Establish Your Own Dress Code for Your Kids.

Unfortunately, wearing the wrong colored shirt to school could get a kid killed nowadays. Gangs rely on clothing colors to identify their friends as well as their enemies. A child who is unaware of this fact could become a victim of gang vengeance.

In addition, kids have to fear being mugged or robbed for their clothing and jewelry. There have been several cases of kids being assaulted or murdered for a pair of tennis shoes. Certainly, kids who wear expensive clothing or jewelry to school are taking unnecessary risks.

It's imperative for parents to closely monitor what their kids wear to school. It's also extremely important to know about gang colors in order to help your kids avoid wearing clothing that could jeopardize their safety. It's a sad situation, to be sure. But like it or not, it's a reality of life. Crime is depriving our kids of many of the personal freedoms we used to take for granted.

WHAT YOU CAN DO

❑ Learn the school dress code and encourage your kids to dress accordingly. This may be difficult with older kids, but you have to make them understand that you are trying to look out for their best interests. ***Note:*** Some schools have gone so far as to institute a uniform dress policy where all kids dress the same each day. This policy is tantamount to having kids wear a uniform like "prep school" students have worn for generations. In addition to simplifying the problem of what a kid should wear to school, it helps reduce the incidence of crime by eliminating some of the motivating forces behind it. If your school is faced with escalating crime, talk to school officials and parent groups about implementing a uniform dress program for your school.

❑ Get information about gang colors from the police department and school officials so you'll have a better idea of what colors your kids should avoid. Most local law enforcement agencies have a gang task force with specialists who understand the workings of various gangs. It's a good idea to consult with the task force in your area. They can provide the most current information about what kids can do to avoid problems with gangs.

❑ Don't let your kids wear expensive clothing or jewelry to school. A show of wealth or affluence could cause your kids to be targeted by a mugger or street gang. Also, it's too easy for such items to mysteriously disappear during the course of the school day, particularly during P.E. when clothing and jewelry are left in gym locker rooms.

❑ Don't put your child's name where it's visible on clothing, backpacks, bikes and the like. When your child's name is showing, a molester has a valuable piece of information: the child's name. That makes it much easier for the molester, since he can approach your child as though he knows him. Most molesters are masters of deceit and cunning. Even a child who has been trained not to talk to strangers can fall victim if he's tricked into thinking the molester is someone the family knows.

27. Teach Your Kids to Be "Street Smart."

If kids are going to survive in today's world, they must be taught the realities of life at a very early age. Naiveté can put them in great danger. This is not to say you should frighten them out of their wits. As stated earlier in this book, there are many ways to teach your kids safety skills in a positive, even entertaining, manner (see page 53).

Most of these skills are aimed at dealing with adults. However, your child's first encounter with crime most likely will involve the neighborhood or schoolyard bully who extorts money or takes your child's possessions. Today's young toughs may threaten with knives or guns instead of fists, so they can be just as dangerous as adults. Coping with bullies can be more difficult than situations involving adults since peer pressure and hurt feelings often get in the way of making sound judgments. It takes a great deal of self-control for a child to resist reacting to the threats and challenges of another kid, so it's important that you constantly remind your children that they are so worthy that they do not need to prove themselves to others. Standing and fighting should be a last resort.

WHAT YOU CAN DO

❑ Make sure young children know their full name, address and phone number, as well as your first and last name, before they start school. They should also know how to use the telephone and how to dial 911 or "0" in an emergency.

❑ Create a special code word, known only to you and your kids, that is to be used in an emergency. Your child should ask for this code word from anyone who claims to have been sent by you to pick up the child. Of course, if you had indeed asked someone to pick up your child for some reason, you would have given the person the code word to use. Your child should be taught never to leave with a person who doesn't know the code. Also, your child should carefully guard the code word and never tell it to anyone, including friends. You should change the code word periodically, just to be sure.

❑ Your child should know to be suspicious of any adult who asks for his or her assistance. Such an occurrence should be like a warning bell to your child. Adults should only seek help from other adults. It's inappropriate for adults to seek help from children. Molesters often use the ploy of asking a child to help locate a lost puppy or toy. In fact, it's one of their favorite lures, mainly because it works so well. Many young children simply have not been taught the proper safety skills to be able to recognize such traps.

❑ Help your children understand that they don't always have to do what adults say. This may contradict many of the things we teach our kids about being polite and respecting adults. However, children certainly have the right to question the authority of any adult when it does not conform to the safety skills they have learned.

❑ Children must learn to trust their instincts. If a situation makes them feel uncomfortable, they should move away from it as quickly and as safely as they can. Most children realize when a situation isn't quite right, and they should know that it is acceptable to act on their feelings.

❑ Teach your children the importance of using the buddy system. They should never go anywhere without a friend or companion. Children are far more vulnerable when they are alone.

❑ Children should always make it a rule to walk on the side of the street facing oncoming traffic whenever it is safe to do so. This will help prevent someone from following in a car, then pulling alongside and dragging them into the vehicle. If kids think they're being followed by someone in a car, they should change direction immediately. Should the car turn around to follow, the kids should change direction again and run for safety.

❑ Your kids must know how to react if they happen to be accosted by a stranger. Make sure your kids understand the following basic rules:

• Yell loudly and clearly. However, don't just scream and struggle, since that might look like a child throwing a temper tantrum. Instead, your child should yell specific warnings like, "Help me, that's not my Mommy/Daddy."

• Sit down if possible. It's much harder to drag someone who is on the floor.

• Stay focused and look for opportunities to get away. Your child should do anything possible to avoid being forced into a car with a stranger.

• If there's an opportunity to run for it, your child should drop everything and take off.

❑ In the case of bullies and street gangs, the best defense is to try to avoid them altogether. Help your kids plan routes they have to travel that circumvent the turf of bullies and gangs. If your kids can stay out of the bully's way, the bully loses. Of course, changing routes to avoid danger isn't always possible, so it may be necessary for you to accompany your kids in certain situations.

❑ Teach your child verbal skills using assertive and humorous techniques that deprive the bully of the reward of humiliating someone.

❑ Sometimes, ignoring a bully and walking away can be an effective response. But every situation is different, and your child will have to evaluate the dangers involved in trying to walk away.

❑ In some cases, it's effective if young children build alliances with other kids their age to present a united front against an older bully. Standing together and saying "no" can be a formidable deterrent in some cases. But your kids should be cautioned not to try to fight back when they are threatened with serious injury or feel overwhelmed by the situation. All in all, they should react to a bully as they would to any dangerous person. The objective is to get away as quickly and safely as possible and call for help.

❑ Encourage your child to make friends and socialize at school. The most severe harassment is directed at "loners."

❑ If your child becomes the target of a bully, inform the school immediately. Keep a written record of times, dates, names and circumstances so you can show a pattern of harassment. Urge your school to adopt a clear conduct code that bars verbal humiliation and physical intimidation at school and on school buses.

SUPPLEMENTAL READING

How to Raise a Street Smart Child, by Grace Hechinger

Why Is Everybody Always Picking on Me? A Guide to Handling Bullies for Young People, by Terrence Webster Doyle

28. Make Your Kids Aware of the Dangers of Rape and Sexual Harassment.

Sexual harassment of females often begins as early as the first grade. A child's natural curiosity about the opposite sex sometimes manifests itself in hugging, kissing and fondling, oftentimes against the wishes of the recipient. While such actions may seem innocent at an early age, they can develop into something much more serious as children grow older. Sexual innuendoes, catcalls, fondling and groping are just some of the unpleasant things young girls have to cope with at school. Many girls encounter sexual harassment of some sort throughout their school years. Males who commit such acts demonstrate an arrogant disrespect for the rights of others.

Rape is perhaps the ultimate form of disrespect. Few crimes make a person feel more violated or exploited.

More than half of all rapes are committed by a date or acquaintance. Girls in junior and senior high school are particularly vulnerable. This is the time in their lives when they begin to assert their independence. Yet even the most sophisticated among them rarely have the social skills to deal with the pressures of sexual experimentation. In a recent survey, most high school boys said they expected sexual favors when they took a girl on a date, especially if they spent money on the girl. This is a scary revelation. No wonder we are seeing more sexual harassment in our high schools, younger rapists and an epidemic of teen pregnancy.

WHAT YOU CAN DO

❑ Teach your children respect for others and for themselves! Begin at an early age. People who respect life rarely violate other people.

❑ Be open and honest on the topic of sex. Your kids are sure to have questions. Don't avoid the issue. Give your kids truthful answers based on your values and views. If you refuse to discuss the topic, you might force your kids to go elsewhere and possibly get all the wrong answers.

• Explain to your kids that sexual curiosity is normal, but that sexual contact only takes place between consenting partners. Any contact that isn't consensual is inappropriate. If a person is forced or coerced into any sexual activity, he or she has been sexually assaulted as defined by law.

• Help your kids understand that responsibility goes hand in hand with sex. Explain that this is one reason sexual intercourse should not occur until adulthood, ideally between married partners.

• Teach your kids that abstinence until marriage not only is acceptable, but is also preferable. Kids are experimenting with sex earlier than we would like to believe, some even in their pre-teens. This can put a lot of pressure on kids to "go along," while reinforcing the attitude in some boys that they have a right to have sex (since "everybody else is doing it").

❑ Be aware that your daughter is far more vulnerable to rape by a date or acquaintance than by a stranger. Among high school and college female rape victims, more than 80% knew their attacker. This statistic is based solely upon reported rapes. Many date rapes are never reported, so this percentage might actually be much higher.

❑ When a girl first begins dating, she should always try to go on double dates to ensure that other people are around. The same is true if she goes on a blind date or out with any boy for the first time. A girl should avoid being alone with any boy she doesn't know very well. It should be a warning to the girl if the boy is overly anxious to get her alone.

❑ While some girls start unchaperoned dating as young as 13 or 14, you are the best judge of when your daughter should be allowed to date. Maturity and responsibility are more important than age. Don't be pressured into allowing your daughter to date just because she insists that other girls her age are doing it. Generally, girls who faze into dating at chaperoned events (where the parents drive the girl and her date to and from events) are more confident about unchaperoned dating.

❑ It's a good idea to have your daughter go "Dutch" treat on casual dates. If a boy pays all the expenses, he might get the idea that he's entitled to have sex, even against his date's will.

❑ A girl should always make it clear early on the date what she does and does not wish to do regarding intimate contact. Boys who receive such direct communications have a better idea of what to expect from a date and are less inclined to force themselves on a girl. This is not meant to imply that a girl is ever to blame if she is raped.

❑ Never let your daughter socialize alone with a group of boys. Girls should be especially careful after sporting events, which can heighten feelings of aggression and hysteria that might lead to anti-social or criminal behavior. The threat of gang rape is much greater during these and similar events.

❑ Don't let your daughter attend parties or other social gatherings which are predominantly male. There have been too many tragic stories of girls who were lured to such parties which turned into gang rapes. No matter how flattering it may seem, a girl should always be suspicious of the attention of a group of boys.

❑ A girl should never accept a ride home or an invitation for a late night snack from someone she has just met.

❑ Make sure your daughter understands the dangers of being under the influence of drugs or alcohol. Nearly 75% of the males and 55% of the females involved in acquaintance rape had been drinking or taking drugs before the attack.

❑ Teach your daughter what to do if she fears being raped while on a date. There are a number of good books on the topic, including those listed below. Check with your librarian for additional recommendations.

❑ Encourage your daughter to report any sexual harassment. Such behavior should never be tolerated regardless of where it occurs or the circumstances involved.

SUPPLEMENTAL READING

What Every Woman Needs to Know About Sexual Assault, by Richard W. Eaves

I Never Called it Rape, by Robin Warshaw

Rape: What Would You Do If...?, by Dianna Daniels Booher

The Facts About Rape, by Jo Ann Bren Guernsey

29. Carefully Screen and Monitor Your Kids' Day-Care Center.

Changes in the American family over the last 50 years have culminated in a life-style that puts many young children at greater risk of sexual or physical abuse. Today, fewer than 20% of American families fit the classical configuration of a father who goes off to work and a mother who stays home to care for the children. More typical is the family where both parents go off to work, or the family with only one parent heading the household who must work out of the home to support the children. In either case, the children must be tended by relatives, baby-sitters or day-care centers.

In recent years, some day-care centers have received a great deal of negative publicity. Shocking cases of sexual and physical abuse have surfaced with alarming frequency. Perhaps most frightening about such abuse is the large number of children who are victimized, the long period of time during which the abuse occurs and the length of time it takes to detect the abuse.

If you have to entrust your children to a day-care center, it is imperative that you find the finest and safest available. But just because you believe the facility to be excellent, you cannot afford to drop your guard. You must maintain your vigilance and constantly monitor the situation at any day-care center you choose. You can never take for granted that your child is completely safe in any day-care facility, regardless of how reputable it may seem.

WHAT YOU CAN DO

❑ Use only day-care centers that are fully licensed and accredited.

❑ Inquire about how thoroughly the facility checks the qualifications and references of its staff, as well as what system is used for background checks. Every staff member should have undergone a check of police records for any prior charges or convictions.

❑ The staff-to-child ratio should be adequate, usually about one staff member to four children ages three years and younger and one staff member to seven kids four and up.

❑ Inquire about discipline. The staff should never be allowed to administer any form of physical or mental punishment to discipline children.

❑ Before you select a day-care center, visit the facility to observe the operation while children are engaged in their usual routine so that you are satisfied with the level of care they receive.

❑ Never use a day-care center that prohibits unscheduled visits by parents. You should be welcome to visit the facility unannounced at any time.

❑ All areas of the facility should be accessible to you at all times. Never leave your kids with a facility that has any area that is "off limits" to parents.

❑ Make it a standing rule that your child is never allowed to be taken off the premises by anyone, staff or otherwise, without your permission.

❑ The facility's policy for preventing child abuse should be discussed openly. If administrators have no policy or seem uncomfortable about discussing it, you should find another day-care center.

❑ Take an active interest in the facility. Spend as much time there as your schedule permits. Your involvement can help head off any problems before they get started. Take note of any major shifts in the staff and find out why they occurred. You have a right to know about anything that affects the safety of your children.

❑ Never ignore negative reports about the facility. You should immediately investigate. If you have any doubts whatsoever, find another day-care center.

❑ Talk to your child every day about his or her day-care experiences. If you have the slightest suspicion about any improprieties, investigate further, and if necessary, find another facility.

❑ Children who are afraid of returning to a day-care center after a reasonable period of adjustment should be removed from the program and placed in a different facility. If the fears persist, child counseling may be needed to determine the cause.

❑ Immediately investigate any injuries or bruises that can't be reasonably explained. Be suspicious of any recurring bumps or bruises.

❑ When your kids are old enough to learn, teach them about private parts of the body (see page 51) and other safety skills for preventing sexual abuse (see page 48).

SUPPLEMENTAL READING

55 Ways to Evaluate Your Child-Care Options and Gain Peace of Mind, by Jan Dargatz

Family Friendly Child-Care, by Susan Kettmann

SPECIAL OCCASIONS, HOLIDAYS, SHOPPING AND TRAVELING

It's another sad commentary on our world, but there simply is no place our kids can go to avoid the dangers of crime. And there is no season without violence. We're a long way from having peace on Earth.

While it's necessary to watch over your kids in everyday life, you also must take special precautions during certain holidays and while traveling or shopping. Even though kidnapping by a stranger is relatively rare, it is still something you must contend with each time you leave home with your kids. Children, like adults, are far more vulnerable when they are on unfamiliar ground. If your child gets lost or separated from you at a parade, shopping mall or airport, he or she obviously could be in great danger.

Child molesters are extremely adept at luring young children away. Children who have not been taught the appropriate safety skills are no match at all for a molester. It can take a molester less than a minute to convince an unwary child to leave with him. Children who know what to do when confronted by such a person stand a much better chance of coming away unharmed.

But never forget how shrewd and devious many molesters are. Some manage to avoid detection their entire lives. So regardless of how well-trained your kids are, they can still be vulnerable. Children who are closely watched and supervised by their parents are the safest of all.

30. Take Special Precautions on Halloween.

Halloween should be a fun time for children, yet almost every year,tragic incidents occur. We've all heard the news stories about trick-or-treat candy and fruit containing everything from drugs to glass slivers, razor blades and needles. Many parents no longer let their children go trick-or-treating. Instead, they organize neighborhood parties and hay rides with plenty of adult supervision. Regardless of what activities you deem appropriate for your children, there are a number of precautions you should take.

WHAT YOU CAN DO

❑ Do not let children go trick-or-treating alone. Young children should be accompanied by a parent or responsible adult. Older kids should be allowed to go only with a group of friends.

❑ Do not allow children of any age to go trick-or-treating outside your immediate neighborhood. Better yet, arrange a trick-or-treat "cooperative" with your neighbors, whereby your kids go only to those homes in the cooperative. Each household marks the treats with identification stickers or labels so you'll know where your child gets each item.

❑ Always know the exact route your child will be taking. Insist that your child take only the route you have approved beforehand.

❑ Warn your kids not to knock or ring the doorbell of houses where the lights are out. They should only go to those houses with a porch light on. (Make sure your own home is well-lit to indicate trick-or-treaters are welcome.)

❑ Insist that your children respect the property rights and privacy of others. Not only is it the responsible thing to do, it's also the safest. Don't forget, many individuals have armed themselves. Even the pettiest of pranks could cause a trigger-happy person to over-react.

❑ Set and enforce a strict curfew, and make sure you or a responsible adult will be at home at this pre-arranged time. Your kids probably should be back at home by nine o'clock at the latest.

❑ Inspect all candy and other treats that your children bring home. Throw out anything that is unwrapped or looks suspicious.

❑ Notify the police immediately if you find anything dangerous in the treats your kids bring home.

❑ If you live in a high-crime area or in a neighborhood with a lot of gang activity, the safest thing to do is find an alternative to trick-or-treating. Try to plan a party or other activities instead. On a night when it's acceptable to wear masks and costumes that conceal identities, it's much too tempting for muggers and gangs to take advantage of the situation.

31. Take Special Precautions during the Holidays.

The holiday season should also be a joyous time for children, and most of the time it is. Yet it can also be a time of great danger for our kids. We all have a tendency to lower our guard somewhat during the holidays. We become more trusting and open with strangers. We spend more time away from home on shopping trips with throngs of other shoppers or traveling to visit friends and family. Without the proper safeguards, it's easy for kids and grown-ups alike to be victimized during the holidays.

WHAT YOU CAN DO

❑ Be careful about leaving young children at temporary child-care centers in malls and shopping centers. You're probably better off arranging for your own baby-sitter to watch your children at home.

❑ Watch your kids closely while shopping during the holidays (see page 141). Never leave young children to browse in the toy section while you shop in another part of the store. Many child molesters routinely hang out in toy stores waiting for the right opportunity to lure a child away.

❑ Be equally cautious about leaving older kids in mall arcades while you shop. These places are also frequent haunts of some child molesters.

❑ Always accompany young children to public rest rooms. Never leave them there alone.

❑ Make sure your children know exactly what to do if they get lost or separated from you (see page 143).

❑ Keep car doors locked and the windows rolled up when you're driving to and from shopping areas. Carjackers and purse snatchers are very active during the holidays.

❑ Park only in well-lit, highly visible sections of the parking lot. And always make a mental note of where you park. You don't want to have to wander around the parking lot looking for your car, especially if you're loaded down with packages and have the kids in tow.

❑ When you return to your car, take a look before you get inside to make sure that an assailant isn't hiding on the floorboard.

❑ Keep your purse and packages out of sight in the car trunk or on the floorboard. If thieves can't see your possessions, they're less likely to strike.

❑ Never leave young children unattended in your car while you go inside a store, even if you only plan to be in the store for a minute or so.

❑ Never let young children hold your purse or carry packages. This makes a tempting target for a purse or package snatcher. Your child could be injured if such an attempt were made.

❑ Remember, Santa Claus can be intimidating to some kids. If your child is reluctant to sit on Santa's knee, do not force him or her to do so, since this might go counter to your teachings about being cautious around strangers. Many times, if you let the child observe Santa with the other kids, he or she will eventually work up the courage to talk to Santa voluntarily.

❑ Avoid buying children's toys and video games that depict violence. Some toy guns are so realistic that it's difficult to distinguish them from the real thing. This could prove to be extremely dangerous if a child carries such a toy to school or to the playground.

32. *Keep Young Children in View at All Times When You Take Them Shopping.*

Shopping with children can be difficult and trying. Kids often get bored and try to find ways to amuse themselves. Sometimes they wander off or lag behind and get separated from a parent who is preoccupied with shopping. You certainly don't expect this to happen, but you have to be prepared for such an occurrence nonetheless. It's imperative that your kids know what to do if they get lost or separated from you.

In some cases, a child is allowed to wait in the toy or book department while the parent shops elsewhere in the store. Also, when kids get a little older, parents sometimes let them stay in video arcades or game rooms. As stated earlier, either of these can be risky for children, since these are two of the places child molesters often go to find their victims. Remember, child molesters are very adept at convincing children, even young teens, to leave the premises with them.

Kidnappers and child abductors who prey on infants also frequent shopping centers and malls. They know that parents might be distracted just long enough for them to make their move. You have to be on full alert every time you take your kids shopping.

WHAT YOU CAN DO

❑ If you have an infant with you, use a back-pack or front-pack halter-seat to carry the baby close to your body. Try to avoid putting your baby in an infant carrier strapped onto a shopping cart. This makes it much easier for someone to take your child if you're not watching closely.

❑ If you have to put your toddler in a shopping cart, make sure the child is strapped in and well-secured. Not only will this reduce the possibility of your child falling out of the cart, it will also make it more difficult for someone to remove the child.

❑ When shopping with older kids, try to bring along a toy or game that will help keep them occupied while you shop.

❑ If your children are old enough, give each of them a responsibility, such as pushing the shopping cart or helping you locate products on the shelves. This will help occupy their time, and at the same time, will help keep them close to you. However, do not let young children carry your purse or packages. Your child might be injured if a thief tries to snatch the items and run.

❑ Don't let a child lag behind. If he or she gets too tired to keep up or becomes extremely bored, take a short break, or cut the trip short and come back another time.

❑ Never leave a child in one part of the store while you shop elsewhere. Remember, child molesters and kidnappers have been known to hang around toy and book departments waiting for the right child to come along.

❑ Always have a plan for the possibility that your child will get lost or separated. Your child must know *exactly* what to do in such a situation.

- In most cases, it's best to instruct your children to simply stay put (unless they feel they are in danger). Instruct them to remain in the area where they were separated from you. This will make it easier for you to backtrack and locate them. They will be far more difficult to find once they leave the area to look for you.

- As a back-up, establish a pre-arranged meeting place where your lost child can go if he or she feels threatened while waiting for you to return. Bear in mind, however, that some large shopping malls are like mazes, and it's very easy for a child to get turned around or lose his or her sense of direction. Try to choose a location that you are confident your child can find. Of course, any such decision will be determined by the age and maturity of your child.

- Your children should not waste time trying to find you. They should either stay put or proceed directly to a pre-arranged meeting place if they can locate it without getting lost. If they cannot find the meeting place, they should try to find a policeman, security guard or store clerk and tell that person that they are lost.

• If the child cannot locate someone of authority, he or she should go to a pay phone and call home, call a phone friend, or call the police. Make sure your child knows exactly whom he or she should call in such a situation and that he or she knows the phone number. If the pre-arranged meeting place is near a pay phone, it will make it easier for your child to find a phone and call for help.

• Put a label with the name, address and phone number of your children inside their clothing to help the police locate you if it becomes necessary.

• *Children should know that they are never to leave the premises with any adult for any reason until you have been located.*

33. Teach Your Kids Safety Skills for Using Public Transportation.

Most transit authorities go to great lengths to provide security for their riders. Some transit systems use everything from surveillance cameras to armed guards to prevent crime. Unfortunately, these security measures don't always deter criminals. Pickpockets, muggers, rapists and child molesters sometimes find easy prey on buses and trains. In this day and age, it's absolutely imperative that your kids know the fundamental safety skills for using public transportation.

WHAT YOU CAN DO

❑ Ride the line with your kids several times to make sure they are familiar with the route and know which stops to exit and enter the bus. If your kids have to transfer, make sure they know the correct procedure and the right point to make the transfer.

❑ Plan the safest route for your kids to use when going to and from the bus stop. It's a good idea to walk the route with them the first time or two. Make sure they know the location of safe places along the way where they can go if they feel threatened or in danger. Unless they are compelled to do otherwise, they should walk facing oncoming traffic and keep a safe distance from vehicles parked on the street. They also should try to keep away from shrubs, isolated areas, vacant lots and alleys along the route, and stay in well-lit areas as much as possible.

❑ Try to arrange for your kids to walk with other kids or responsible adults when going to and from the bus stop. Make sure your kids use highly visible, well-lit stops.

❑ Never let kids wait in entranceways to houses or apartments where they could be dragged inside. And don't let them stand near the curb where they could be pulled into a car. They should either stand in the middle of the sidewalk or with their backs to a wall. They should stay alert to what is going on around them at all times!

❑ When kids get on the bus, they should take a seat as close to the driver as possible. They should avoid sitting at the very rear of the bus, even if they have to stand.

❑ If your kids feel threatened by the actions of another passenger, they should immediately move to a position by the driver, even if they have to remain standing. If the threat continues, your kids should ask for the driver's assistance.

❑ Obviously, your kids should know that they are never to get off the bus with a stranger or exit the bus at other than their normal stop unless they are following the directions of the driver during an emergency.

❑ If your kids have to ride a subway or train, teach them to wait near the token booth until the train arrives. They should never stand near the edge of the platform.

❑ Instruct your kids to enter one of the middle cars of the train and sit or stand as near the exit as possible. They should try to stay in the vicinity of other people. They should avoid sitting alone in any car.

34. Watch Your Kids Closely in Airports, Bus Depots and Train Stations.

It's important to exercise great care when you travel with your kids. Transportation facilities in general, and airports in particular, are usually jammed with travelers. Most of them are decent people concerned only with getting to their destination. However, some of these people have criminal intent, especially during peak travel times when there's more rushing and confusion than normal. If your kids get lost or separated from you, they could be at great risk. The problem is compounded by the fact that many airports are sprawling, confusing complexes that are difficult to navigate, particularly when you have kids with you.

WHAT YOU CAN DO

❑ Try to arrive at the terminal early. When you're rushed, you're more likely to drop your guard.

❑ If at all possible, get maps of the airport in advance from the airline or your travel agent. This will make it much easier to get to the right gate.

❑ Try to have someone drive you to the terminal and drop you off by the entrance. If skycaps are available, check your luggage at curbside to simplify the check-in process. It's always a good idea to check in early in case you have to resolve any problems concerning your flight or other travel arrangements.

❑ Check as much of your luggage as possible. Carry only the bare necessities in your carry-on bags. This will eliminate some of the distractions, enabling you to concentrate on your kids.

❑ Make your kids aware of the importance of staying close by you at all times.

❑ Stay with your kids the entire time you are waiting for your flight. Accompany them to the rest rooms, the gift shop, game room or snack bar. Never let them go off alone.

❑ Put your name, address and phone number, along with your flight number and destination, on a label *inside* your kids' clothing. This could help the authorities locate you if your child were to get lost or separated from you.

❑ Do not let young kids carry handbags or packages. Here again, this might be a tempting target for a purse snatcher. Similarly, never leave kids alone to watch luggage and other valuables while you go to the rest room, snack bar, etc.

❑ Try to ensure that your kids are seated next to you on the plane. Although this is sometimes difficult during peak travel periods, most airlines will do their best to accommodate parents traveling with children.

❑ Always take advantage of pre-boarding privileges. This will allow you to get your kids safely on board and settled in their seats ahead of the rush.

❑ When you reach your destination, watch your kids closely while you're claiming your bags. If at all possible, have a skycap claim your bags while you watch your kids. Here again, in the rush and confusion of a large crowd, it would be easy for an abductor to make off with a child. Remember, traveling can be just as disorienting for children as it can be for adults. Keep your kids close by at all times.

❑ Try to pre-arrange transfers from the terminal to your hotel. The safest thing to do is have a friend or relative pick you up at the terminal. If that isn't possible, try to use a shuttle bus that goes directly from the terminal to your hotel or other drop-off point.

❑ Avoid picking up a rental car at the terminal unless you are very familiar with the city. All too often, airports, bus depots and train stations are located in remote or undesirable parts of the city. Your safest bet is to have the rental company deliver your car to your hotel.

- ❑ Never get into an unmarked "taxi." Make sure the cab is clearly marked as such and that the driver's identification and photo are clearly displayed.

- ❑ Beware of sharing taxi rides with strangers.

- ❑ Make sure your kids know the name of your destination city, as well as the name, address and phone number where you're staying.

35. Keep a Close Eye on Your Kids While Staying in a Hotel.

Like airport terminals, hotels are filled with strangers coming and going at all hours. In airports, however, travelers usually are more alert to potential dangers. This is not always the case with hotels. Many people tend to lower their guard once they reach the supposedly safe confines of a hotel. This false sense of security can be hazardous to you and your kids.

At hotels in and around theme parks and other attractions catering to families, many people falsely assume that the hotel provides adequate security and protection for kids. This is rarely the case. As always, it is up to parents to provide for the protection and security of their children.

WHAT YOU CAN DO

❑ Inquire about a hotel's safety and security before you reserve your room. Ask about the types of locks used (there should be at least one deadbolt lock on guest room doors), whether the doors have peepholes, access to the hotel after hours, security guards and security cameras. Also, ask if guest rooms have outside entrances. Ideally, your room should not open to the outside but to a well-lit, secure interior hallway that's relatively short. If you aren't convinced your family will be safe, you're better off finding another hotel.

❑ Don't drop your guard in hotels, even so-called luxury hotels. It is very difficult for hotels to provide adequate security for adult guests, let alone children. With hundreds of total strangers checking in and out of a hotel each week, it's impossible for the hotel staff to know who is a guest and who isn't.

❑ Never let young children stay in a separate room. If your family requires more than one room, try to get two adjoining rooms with a door that opens between them. If that isn't possible, it may be necessary to double up in one room. Most hotels have roll-away beds that can be brought into a room to accommodate families with children.

❑ Keep your hotel room locked the entire time you are in your room. Use every lock on the door.

❑ Make sure that doors between rooms are locked at all times. The same is true of sliding glass doors and windows to the outside.

❑ Carry a door wedge or portable travel lock for extra security on your hotel room door. Most of these devices are relatively inexpensive and compact enough to carry in your suitcase. For an extra measure of safety, carry a portable intrusion/fire alarm as well. In the absence of such a device, prop a chair against the inside of your door before you go to sleep.

❑ Do not let children answer the door if someone knocks. Use the peephole or talk through the closed door to identify the person at the door. Never open your hotel room door unless you know the person is supposed to be there (a guest you're expecting, room service, etc.).

❑ Never leave young children alone in the room when you go out. And be very cautious about using babysitters provided by hotels. Your best bet is to plan all activities so that your children are with you at all times.

❑ Supervise your kids closely during the entirety of your stay. Do not let youngsters go to game rooms, vending machines, swimming pools or dining rooms unless you accompany them.

SUPPLEMENTAL READING

Your Guide to Safe Travel in the U.S.A., by Richard W. Eaves

Trouble-Free Travel with Children, by Vicki Lansky

36. Plan for Every Eventuality When Kids Must Travel Alone.

In an ideal world, kids would never have to travel alone. Unfortunately, in these times of joint custody and court-ordered visits, parents often have no other choice. Sending a child off on a trip alone can be an ordeal filled with anxiety for both parents and the child. And for good reason. Anyone who has ever traveled knows that it can be a taxing experience filled with uncertainties. Flights get canceled; connecting flights are delayed; boarding gates get changed. Even seasoned travelers have difficulty navigating airport terminals. Imagine what it could be like for your child traveling alone. You can hope for a smooth trip, but you should plan for every situation that might arise.

Perhaps most unnerving is the fact that you are temporarily putting your child's safety in the hands of total strangers. People you have never met will be responsible for your child the moment he or she steps on board. The safety skills you have taught your child, particularly those involving interaction with adults, will be of paramount importance.

Naturally, the decision to let your child travel alone will be determined by his or her age and maturity, as well as the mode of transportation involved. Children younger than eight or nine probably shouldn't be allowed to travel by themselves on an airline trip that involves multiple plane changes, or take long bus or train trips alone. On such trips, kids not only have to contend with boredom and fatigue, but also the risk of meeting up with a mugger or molester who might try to lure them away at the next stop.

As a rule, bus and train lines can't provide as much supervision for kids traveling alone as airlines, especially on nonstop flights. Buses and trains usually make multiple stops along the way, with passengers boarding and departing on different legs of the trip. This exposes your child to more and more strangers, some of whom might be willing to take advantage of a youngster traveling alone.

We highly recommend that you check with the bus or train line about their policies before you allow your child to travel alone. Unless you're very comfortable with the situation, you should try to make other arrangements.

Children traveling alone has become a common sight on airlines. It's so common, in fact, that some airlines even have frequent flyer clubs for kids. On most airlines, children can fly solo as long as they are at least five years of age. However, a child this young should not be sent on a first trip alone. You can't be sure how the child will react to flying, so it's a good idea to take one or two flights with your child before sending him or her off alone. But regardless of the experience level of your child, thorough planning is the key to a safer trip. Every eventuality must be carefully considered.

WHAT YOU CAN DO

❑ Check with the individual airlines about their policies concerning unaccompanied children. Most airlines allow children to fly alone if they are at least five years of age. However, some airlines may charge an extra fee for kids 12 and under if a connecting flight is involved. The fee covers the extra paperwork and an escort from gate to gate. Of course, teenagers can probably make their own connections, provided they are experienced air travelers. If not, you can request that an escort be provided.

❑ When you make the reservations, inform the airline that your child will be flying alone. You will need to stipulate the name of an adult to take custody of the child at the destination. Remember, the adult who picks up the child will have to provide identification, so alert the party beforehand to avoid any confusion or delays.

❑ Make sure the person meeting your child upon arrival has your child's itinerary well in advance of the trip so there won't be any mix-ups.

❑ Try to book a nonstop or direct flight for your child. If a connection is necessary, make sure it is not the last connecting flight of the day. Should the connection be canceled or missed, your child might have to spend the night alone in a hotel room (but only after you have been notified by the airline).

❑ If a connecting flight is involved, be sure your child knows exactly what to expect. Your child should know that an airline employee, usually a person in uniform, will escort the child from one gate to the next. However, *your child should know that he or she is not to leave the airport with anyone other than the person meeting him or her at the final destination.* In the unlikely event the last connecting flight is missed or canceled, insist that the airline call for your permission before taking the child from the airport.

❑ Arrange your schedule so that you're available by phone until your child has safely reached the final destination. Have the person meeting your child call to let you know that your child has arrived safely.

❑ Give your child specific instructions about what to do if he or she accidentally gets separated from the escort. The safest procedure is to stay put and wait for the escort to backtrack to find the child.

❑ When you make reservations, request a special child's meal. Special meals don't cost extra, but you have to order them at least 24 hours in advance. Naturally, the idea is to make the flight as comfortable and pleasant as possible to help allay some of the anxiety and fear.

❑ If your child has never flown before, take a field trip to the airport to run through the routine. Rehearse the entire procedure, from check-in to baggage claim. Discuss what will happen during the flight, from take-off to landing. Point out or introduce your child to flight attendants and gate attendants so your child will be more familiar with their uniforms and identification tags. Try to cover every detail so your child will be more familiar with the procedure.

❑ On the day of the flight, try to get to the airport early enough to complete the check-in process at least an hour before the flight departs. This will help ensure that everything is in order before your child leaves. It's too easy to overlook something if you're rushed.

❑ Check as much baggage as possible. Try to limit carry-on luggage to one or two small bags that can be stowed under the seat rather than the overhead bin. One of these should be a "busy bag" with items like books, word games, snacks, video games, etc., to help make the trip more comfortable for your child.

❑ Make sure your child has the name, address and phone number of the person who will meet him or her at the destination, as well as a list of names and phone numbers of other responsible adults to call in the event something unexpected happens and you can't be reached. Also, make sure your child has a written itinerary that shows all connecting flights. These items can be carried easily in a neck pouch on a cord that can be worn underneath the child's shirt or blouse. Be sure to include some cash and change for pay phones.

❑ Make sure your child knows how to use pay phones and how to make a long-distance phone call. The newer, coinless machines often found in airports can be confusing, so it's a good idea to teach your kids how to use such phones.

SUPPLEMENTAL READING

How to Fly for Kids! by Natalie Windsor

The PennyWhistle Traveling with Kids Book, by Meredith Brokaw and Annie Gilbar

By Land, By Air, By Sea, by Steve and Ruth Bennett